W9-AYE-303

Grade **1**

Scott Foresman

The Grammar & Writing Book

ISBN: 0-328-14635-8

All Rights Reserved. Printed in the United States of America. This publication is protected by Copyright, and permission should be obtained from the publisher prior to any prohibited reproduction, storage in a retrieval system, or transmission in any form by any means, electronic, mechanical, photocopying, recording, or likewise. For information regarding permission(s), write to: Permissions Department, Scott Foresman, 1900 East Lake Avenue, Glenview, Illinois 60025.

7 8 9 10 V008 09 08 07

PEARSON

Scott
Foresman

Editorial Offices: Glenview, Illinois • Parsippany, New Jersey • New York, New York
Sales Offices: Boston, Massachusetts • Duluth, Georgia • Glenview, Illinois
Coppell, Texas • Sacramento, California • Mesa, Arizona

Table of Contents

Writer's Guide

Rubrics and Models

Check Your Writing

Grammar and Writing Lessons

© Pearson Education

B **Look** at the pictures. **Write** the three sentences in the right order.

Ted scolds the dog.
The trash falls over.
The dog finds the trash.

1. _____

2. _____

3. _____

C **Write** a sentence that tells what could happen next.

4. _____

_____

_____

© Pearson Education

Improving Order/Paragraphs

Original

I went with my mom, dad, and sister. We went to the top of a mountain. We walked around the bottom of the mountain. It had green grass. Finally, we reached the top of the mountain. It was covered with snow. We took a tram to the top. We rode in little cars. It was scary to go so high. We could see really far.

Revising Tips

Put your main idea at the start of the paragraph. (Start with the sentence that says you went to the top of a mountain.)

Put other sentences in order. Tell what happened in order. (The sentences about the tram come before *Finally, we reached the top of the mountain.*)

Use words that tell when. (*Last summer* I went to the top of a mountain. *First* we walked around the bottom of the mountain.)

Write an ending. You might tell how you felt about the trip.

© Pearson Education

Improved

Last summer I went to the top of a mountain. I went with my mom, dad, and sister. First we walked around the bottom of the mountain. It had green grass. Then we took a tram to the top. We rode in little cars. It was scary to go so high. Finally, we reached the top of the mountain. It was covered with snow. We could see really far. We had a great time.

Writer's Corner

Good stories have endings. Write an ending sentence that ties your story together.

© Pearson Education

Voice

Voice is the <u>you</u> in your writing. It shows how you feel.

This sentence does not tell how the writer feels about popcorn.

   We eat popcorn.

This sentence tells how the writer feels about popcorn.

   I just love hot, buttered popcorn!

A **Draw** a line to match the feeling and the picture.

1. sad

2. angry

3. happy

© Pearson Education

B **Match** each sentence with the feeling it shows.
Write the letter on the line.

A excited **B** serious **C** friendly

_____ **1.** Can you come skating with me
on Saturday?

_____ **2.** The new kittens are so cute!

_____ **3.** George Washington was
our first President.

C **Write** about something you do well.
Tell readers how doing it makes you feel.

_____

_____

_____

_____

_____

© Pearson Education

Improving Voice

Original

I play soccer. I like to play. I run up and down the field. I run fast. I wear my soccer shirt. My teammates and I work hard. We like it when our parents watch us play.

Revising Tips

Think about the feeling you want to show. If you are excited about playing soccer, use words that show why you are excited. *(Soccer is my favorite game in the whole world.)*

Keep your readers in mind. Write so that readers can get to know you. *(Sometimes I pretend I am making a goal in the World Cup* shows that you want to be a champion.)

Tell how you feel about your topic. Use words that make word pictures. *(We like it* is dull. *We feel so proud we could burst* makes a picture for readers.)

© Pearson Education

Improved

Soccer is my favorite game in the whole world. Sometimes I pretend I am making a goal in the World Cup. I run up and down the field until I feel dizzy. It is fun wearing my bright green soccer shirt. After a long game, my teammates and I are very tired. When our parents watch us play, we feel so proud we could burst.

Writer's Corner

Do some sentences show how you feel? Read them out loud to see.

© Pearson Education

Word Choice

Good words make your writing interesting. They help readers see what you are saying.

Which tells more about the picture?

plant   curling vine

Curling vine helps readers see the plant.

A **Add** two words from the box to finish the sentence. **Write** the sentence.

| slides | skates | cold | hard |

Jane __ on the __ ice.

© Pearson Education

B **Match** a word from the box with a picture. **Write** the word.

| tiny   bright |

1. _____

2. _____

C **Write** about this picture. **Use** one or more words from the box.

| runs   rides   races |

_____
_____
_____
_____
_____
_____

© Pearson Education

Improving Word Choice

Original

> Bugs are nice. I like to watch them. Bees go around the plants. Butterflies fly over the garden. Little ladybugs go along stems. Worms go on the ground. Spiders make webs between plants.

Revising Tips

Choose exact words. *(roses* instead of *plants)*

Don't use words such as *good* and *nice* too often.   *(Bugs are interesting.* instead of *Bugs are nice.)*

Make word pictures.   *(Worms wiggle on the muddy ground.* instead of *Worms go on the ground.)*

Use clear words.   *(Spiders spin.* instead of *Spiders make.)*

Don't repeat the same word too often.   (Replace *go* in one or two sentences.)

© Pearson Education

Improved

Bugs are interesting. I like to watch them. Bees buzz around the roses. Bright orange and yellow butterflies swirl over the garden. Tiny ladybugs creep along stems. Worms wiggle on the muddy ground. Spiders spin webs between bushes and trees.

Writer's Corner

To make strong word pictures, use words that help the reader hear and see things. *(Bees buzz, bright orange and yellow butterflies)*

© Pearson Education

Sentences

Sentences should make sense. Words should be in the right order.

Not a Sentence   Throws the ball the boy.
Sentence   The boy throws the ball.

Not a Sentence   Falls on the grass.
Sentence   The ball falls on the grass.

A **Circle** the sentence.

1. The boy has.

   Boy a bat has the.

   The boy has a bat.

2. The dog wags his tail.

   Wags his tail.

   Dog tail his the wags.

© Pearson Education

B **Use** a word from the box to write about each picture.

little   fish

1. The ___ jumps.

_____

- -

_____

2. The bird is ___.

_____

- -

_____

C **Write** two sentences about playing outside. **Use** the words below to start the first sentence.

Tim and Ann ___

_____

- -

_____

_____

- -

_____

_____

- -

_____

© Pearson Education

Improving Sentences

Original

My dog Ladyfinger can catch anything. I toss a rubber ball. She catches the ball. In her mouth. I throw little a stick. To my dog. She can catch any stick. I throw a rolled-up sock. Runs across the yard and catches the sock. She brings it back to me. The best dog in the world.

Revising Tips

Make sure each sentence makes sense. *(In her mouth.* does not make sense by itself. *She catches the ball in her mouth.* makes sense.)

Make sure words are in the right order. *(I throw little a stick.* is not in the right order. *I throw a little stick.* is in the right order.)

© Pearson Education

Improved

My dog Ladyfinger can catch anything. I toss a rubber ball. She catches the ball in her mouth. I throw a little stick to my dog. She can catch any stick. I throw a rolled-up sock. My dog runs across the yard and catches the sock. She brings it back to me. Ladyfinger is the best dog in the world.

Writer's Corner

Some sentences tell things. Some sentences ask questions. In your writing, use both kinds of sentences.

© Pearson Education

Rules

There are **rules** that good writers follow. Words are spelled a certain way. Sentences begin with a capital letter. Sentences end with a mark.

can you paly with me
(This doesn't follow the rules.)

Can you play with me?
(This follows the rules.)

A **Circle** the correct word. **Write** the word.

1. Teri ___ the bug. (sees, seez)

_____

- -

_____

2. Can you hit the ___? (bol, ball)

_____

- -

_____

Choose the right end mark. **Write** the sentence.

3. The girl can win (. ?)

_____

- -

_____

© Pearson Education

B **Write** each sentence. **Start** it with a capital letter. **Use** the right end mark.

1. will Mary go

_____

- -

_____

2. a bird is in a tree

_____

- -

_____

C **Write** about a bird you have seen. **Follow** spelling and sentence rules.

_____

- -

_____

- -

_____

- -

_____

- -

_____

- -

_____

© Pearson Education

Improving Rules

Original

What wakes you up each day. Most days
I hear a clock. sometimes I hear a school bus outside.
In summer the berds sing. They are so loud! Some days I
hear rain on the window. Then I no it will be a wet day.
Their are many morning sounds. Which do you like best.

Revising Tips

Check that each sentence begins with a capital letter. *(Sometimes I hear a school bus outside.)*

Make sure each sentence ends with the right mark. *(What wakes you up each day? Which do you like best?)*

Check for spelling mistakes. *(birds instead of berds)*

Check for words that sound the same but are spelled differently. *(I know it will be a wet day. There are many morning sounds.)*

© Pearson Education

Improved

What wakes you up each day? Most days I hear a clock. Sometimes I hear a school bus outside. In summer the birds sing. They are so loud! Some days I hear rain on the window. Then I know it will be a wet day. There are many morning sounds. Which do you like best?

Writer's Corner

Help a friend find mistakes in his or her writing. Your friend can help you find mistakes too.

© Pearson Education

Rubrics and Models

Narrative Writing *Scoring Rubric*

A scoring **rubric** can be used to judge a piece of writing. A rubric is a checklist of traits, or writing skills, to look for. See pages 2–25 to learn more about these traits. Rubrics give a number score for each trait.

	4	**3**	**2**	**1**
Focus/Ideas	Clear ideas on story topic	Good ideas, mostly on story topic	Ideas not always clear or on story topic	Ideas mixed up and not on story topic
Order/ Paragraphs	Strong beginning, middle, and end, with order words	Beginning, middle, and end, with some order words	Missing some parts	Missing many parts
Voice	Writer's feelings about subject clear	Writer interested in subject	Shows little or no feeling	Can't tell how writer feels
Word Choice	Interesting, well-chosen words	Good words	Uses same words or dull words	Uses dull words or wrong words
Sentences	Complete and clear sentences	Most sentences complete and clear	Some sentences not complete or too long	Many sentences not complete or too long
Rules	No mistakes or few mistakes	Some mistakes	Many mistakes	Too many mistakes

Following are four models that are written about a prompt. Each model has been given a score, based on the rubric.

Writing Prompt Write a story about something funny or interesting that happened with a pet.

© Pearson Education

Narrative Writing Model *Score 4*

> One day there was a pet show at the park. Kids were supposed to bring their pets. They would show them off to everyone. I was sad because I didn't have a cat or dog to show. Then my brother said I should take his lizard Fred. It is long and slippery and lives in a cage. So I took Fred to the pet show. Guess what! I won the prize for most unusual pet!

Focus/Ideas   Story built around one clear idea

Order/Paragraphs   Story told in order, with order words *(One day, Then, So)*

Voice   Shows writer's feelings

Word Choice   Interesting words *(long, slippery)*

Sentences   Good, clear sentences

Rules   No mistakes in spelling, grammar, or punctuation

© Pearson Education

Narrative Writing Model *Score 3*

My cat is named Bell. She is fluffy and nice. One day we could not find Bell. We looked in her favrit places. She was not under my bed or in my dad's chair. My dad has a nice big chair. He sits in it after work. Where was Bell? Finely my sister looked in the guraj. Bell was in a dark corner. And not alone! She had two new kittens! And that is where we found Bell.

Focus/Ideas   Most sentences about one idea; some sentences off topic (*My dad has a nice big chair. He sits in it after work.*)

Order/Paragraphs   Moves clearly from beginning to middle to end

Voice   Writer interested in story

Word Choice   Uses some words too much (*nice*)

Sentences   Smooth and interesting

Rules   Some spelling mistakes (*favrit, Finely, guraj*); one sentence not complete (*And not alone!*)

© Pearson Education

Narrative Writing Model *Score 2*

My dog was barking and didn no why so my dad when out there and saw the dog. And then he saw was a big goos. They are allways in our yard in summer it was big and it was squaking at my dog. and that's why my dog was barking.

Focus/Ideas   Some information not part of story idea *(They are allways in our yard in summer.)*

Order/Paragraphs   Needs clearer beginning; some order words

Voice   Few feelings shown

Word Choice   Needs more interesting words

Sentences   Some sentences confusing *(And then he saw was a big goos);* too many ideas in some sentences

Rules   Many spelling mistakes *(didn, no, when, goos, allways, squaking);* mistake with capital letter

© Pearson Education

Narrative Writing Model *Score 1*

> Hapstr got lose and I loked for him and then I could find him and then I give up so my bruther say hed find him. but then my mom gits redy and puts on he shu and theres the hapstr. in the shu. But he was OK so we put him bak in a caj. my bruther could find him ether?

Focus/Ideas Sentences all about one idea, but hard to follow

Order/Paragraphs Information in ending in wrong place; needs clearer ending

Voice No feelings shown

Word Choice Some wrong words *(could, he)*

Sentences Many mixed-up sentences; too many *and*s and *but*s

Rules Many spelling mistakes *(hapstr, lose, loked, bruther, hed, gits, redy, shu, theres, bak, caj, ether)*; mistakes with capital letters and end marks; an incomplete sentence

© Pearson Education

Descriptive Writing *Scoring Rubric*

	4	3	2	1
Focus/Ideas	Clear ideas on topic; very good description	Good description; ideas mostly clear	Description not clear; some parts don't belong	Ideas mixed up or not a description
Order/ Paragraphs	Ideas easy to follow, in order that makes sense	Ideas mostly easy to follow	Order of ideas sometimes confusing	Ideas hard to follow
Voice	Writer's feelings about topic clear	Writer interested in topic	Shows little or no feeling	Can't tell how writer feels
Word Choice	Many word pictures and descriptive words	Some word pictures and descriptive words	Few word pictures; few descriptive words	No word pictures; few descriptive words
Sentences	Sentences complete and clear	Most sentences complete and clear	Some sentences not complete or too long	Many sentences not complete or too long
Rules	No mistakes or few mistakes	Some mistakes	Many mistakes	Too many mistakes

Following are four models that are written about a prompt. Each model has been given a score, based on the rubric.

Writing Prompt Describe a place where things grow. Use strong words to make word pictures.

© Pearson Education

Descriptive Writing Model *Score 4*

The rain forest is a very green place. Millions of plants grow there. That is because it rains so much. Big ferns with huge leaves grow. Flowers grow that don't grow other places. They are very large. Some flowers are bright orange and red. The trees in a rain forest get tall too. You can't see the sky sometimes because the trees are so bushy. The rain forest is a wonderful growing place.

Focus/Ideas   Strong description about one clear idea

Order/Paragraphs   Ideas in an order that is easy to follow; good beginning and ending

Voice   Shows writer's feelings about forest *(The rain forest is a wonderful growing place.)*

Word Choice   Strong word pictures *(Some flowers are bright orange and red.);* good descriptive words *(huge, bushy)*

Sentences   Good, clear sentences

Rules   No mistakes in grammar, spelling, or punctuation

© Pearson Education

Descriptive Writing Model *Score 3*

My grandma has a pretty garden. There are always flowers there. In the spring there are toolups. They look like little red cups. You might think there are no flowers in the fall but there are. There are ornge flowers called mums. And they last almost till winter. In the summer there are roses. She grows yellow and pink and red ones.

Focus/Ideas   All sentences focused on the garden

Order/Paragraphs   Sentences about summer flowers in wrong order; needs clear ending

Voice   Shows interest in topic

Word Choice   Some word pictures *(They look like little red cups.);* could use more descriptive words

Sentences   Most sentences complete; sound good

Rules   A few spelling mistakes *(toolups, ornge)*

© Pearson Education

Descriptive Writing Model *Score 2*

My place where things grow is the forest. They are near my house and there so many trees you wont belive. It is dark in the forest one time I got lost their and nobody found me for a while I was scared that time. The trees in the forest are big. they have many branchs and leafs. Grow tall too.

Focus/Ideas No connection between main idea and sentences about getting lost

Order/Paragraphs Needs strong beginning and ending

Voice Writer's feelings shown

Word Choice Uses dull words *(big, many)*; no word pictures

Sentences Some sentences mixed up; too many ideas in some sentences

Rules Many spelling mistakes or wrong words *(wont, belive, their, branchs, leafs)*; one missing capital letter; one incomplete sentence

© Pearson Education

Descriptive Writing Model *Score 1*

A gaden is nice flors and other grow ther. Blue puple gren and red. but ther also trees but ther not blue or puple. But the gaden is so nice because so many nice flors and other ther.

Focus/Ideas   About a garden, but needs more ideas

Order/Paragraphs   No clear beginning, middle, or end

Voice   Some of writer's feelings shown

Word Choice   A few words describing colors; no word pictures; the word *nice* used too often

Sentences   Many mixed-up sentences; too many *buts*

Rules   Many spelling mistakes *(gaden, flors, ther, puple, gren);* some words left out in first and last sentence; mistake with capital letter; an incomplete sentence

© Pearson Education

Persuasive Writing *Scoring Rubric*

	4	3	2	1
Focus/Ideas	Clear ideas; good reasons used to persuade	Clear ideas; reasons help persuade	Ideas not always clear or do not persuade; few reasons	Ideas not clear or do not persuade
Order/ Paragraphs	Strong beginning and ending; reasons in clear order	Has beginning and ending; reasons in some order	No clear beginning and ending; no clear order to reasons	No beginning and ending
Voice	Writer's feelings about topic clear	Writer interested in topic	Shows little or no feeling	Can't tell how writer feels
Word Choice	Good use of words to persuade	Some words used to persuade	Few words used to persuade	Dull word choice; no words that persuade
Sentences	Sentences complete and clear	Most sentences complete and clear	Some sentences not complete or too long	Many sentences not complete or too long
Rules	No mistakes or few mistakes	Some mistakes	Many mistakes	Too many mistakes

Following are four models that are written about a prompt. Each model has been given a score, based on the rubric.

Writing Prompt Write a letter to your parents. Persuade them to let you do something special. Use the correct letter format.

© Pearson Education

Persuasive Writing Model *Score 4*

Dear Mom and Dad,

    May we go to the museum this weekend? There is a new dinosaur show there. Some kids at school saw it. They said it was awesome! You know I love dinosaurs. We always have a good time on family outings. Also, we are having a dinosaur unit at school. I should learn more about them. The show will help me. Thanks, Mom and Dad!

                Love,

                Terence

Focus/Ideas   Clear ideas; many strong reasons

Order/Paragraphs   Strong beginning and ending

Voice   Shows writer's feelings *(I love dinosaurs.)*

Word Choice   Uses words to persuade *(awesome, should)*

Sentences   Sentences complete, sound good

Rules   No mistakes; follows letter form

© Pearson Education

Persuasive Writing Model *Score 3*

Dear Mom,

    I would like to go out to the pizza place on saturday. I would like to take Stacy and Erin to. We should go on saturday because it is our day off. We all like to eat pizza and play the games there. Maybe we could get a new video game for home. We will lissen to you and we will not get rowdy and we will be happy if you take us.

Love,

Molly

Focus/Ideas   Clear ideas; many reasons; one reason not on the topic *(Maybe we could get a new video game for home.)*

Order/Paragraphs   Good beginning; ending needs to be stronger

Voice   Some feelings shown

Word Choice   Some words to persuade *(should)*

Sentences   Most sentences clear; last sentence with too many *ands*

Rules   Mistake with capital letter *(saturday)*; some spelling mistakes *(to, lissen)*; follows letter form

© Pearson Education

Persuasive Writing Model *Score 2*

Dear Dad,

   Could we play mini golf on friday. Me and Ross like to play. It is fun. Ross and me have played like a hunded times. You us a club and you hit the ball into the hol and then you go to the next one and hit again. Can we please play?

                     Chad

Focus/Ideas Explanation of how to play golf not necessary; needs more reasons

Order/Paragraphs Has clear beginning and end

Voice Writer's feelings shown

Word Choice Unneeded words *(like a hunded times)*; no words to persuade

Sentences Sentence with too many *ands*

Rules Some spelling mistakes *(hunded, us, hol)*; mistake with capital letter *(friday)*; wrong words *(Me and Ross; Ross and me)*; one sentence with wrong end punctuation *(Could we play mini golf on friday.)*; no letter closing

© Pearson Education

Persuasive Writing Model *Score 1*

Dear Mom and dad

How are you? I am fin. I like to get books and then we will read them their for awile and then we will play coputer games and then we will walk home. So can I walk to the libery with Holly after school. she is big enough.

Love

Cara

Focus/Ideas   Main idea not clear; some ideas not about topic

Order/Paragraphs   Beginning not clear about topic of letter; ideas not in order; unclear ending

Voice   Some feelings shown

Word Choice   No words to persuade

Sentences   Mixed-up sentences; long sentence with too many *and*s

Rules   Many spelling mistakes *(fin, their, awile, coputer, libery)*; mistakes with capital letters *(dad, she is big enough)*; mistakes in punctuation (no comma after greeting or closing; no question mark after question)

© Pearson Education

Expository Writing *Scoring Rubric*

	4	3	2	1
Focus/Ideas	Clear topic with many facts; very good explanation	Good explanation; clear ideas with some facts	Explanation not always clear or on topic; few facts	Explanation not clear or on topic; few facts
Order/Paragraphs	Ideas easy to follow	Ideas mostly easy to follow	Ideas not easy to follow	Ideas hard to follow
Voice	Shows writer's feelings, but serious	Shows writer's feelings, but mostly serious	Shows little or no feeling	Writing not serious
Word Choice	Clear, well-chosen words	Words mostly well chosen	Words sometimes don't fit topic	Words often don't fit topic
Sentences	Sentences complete and clear	Most sentences complete and clear	Some sentences not complete or too long	Many sentences not complete or too long
Rules	No mistakes or few mistakes	Some mistakes	Many mistakes	Too many mistakes

Following are four models that are written about a prompt. Each model has been given a score, based on the rubric.

Writing Prompt   Write about a job that grown-ups do. Explain the work they must do each day.

© Pearson Education

Expository Writing Model *Score 4*

Teachers help kids to learn. They teach kids how to read and write. They help kids learn about plants and animals. Kids learn to be kind to each other too. Being a teacher is hard. There are many kids in a class. Sometimes they all raise their hands at once! Teachers have to grade papers and make up lessons. When kids learn new things, they can thank their teachers.

Focus/Ideas Clear explanation with many facts

Order/Paragraphs Good beginning and ending

Voice Friendly but serious voice

Word Choice Exact words (*plants, kind*); good word pictures (*Sometimes they all raise their hands at once!*)

Sentences Sentences complete, sound good

Rules No mistakes in grammar, spelling, or punctuation

© Pearson Education

Expository Writing Model *Score 3*

> Farmers are important. We need farmers to grow food for us. They plant crops like corn or lettis on their land. Then they have to water the crops alot. They pick the crops. Then they send them to a market. So we can buy them. They also grow animals like cows.

Focus/Ideas   Most ideas clear and on topic

Order/Paragraphs   Good beginning; needs strong ending

Voice   Serious voice; could show more feelings

Word Choice   Exact, clear nouns *(corn, lettis)*

Sentences   Most sentences smooth, sound good

Rules   Some spelling mistakes *(lettis, alot);* one incomplete sentence *(So we can buy them)*

© Pearson Education

Expository Writing Model *Score 2*

A docter taks care of peple sick peple and also checkups for well peple. It is a good job because evryone gets sick sometimes plus evryone always needs checkups. he checks you hart and nees. He looks in you ear if you have a ear ake. I had a ear ake last year I went to the docter I have to wait a long time. Finely he asks whats wrong with you. It is a good job for peple to do.

Focus/Ideas   Main idea not always clear; ideas repeated; some ideas not on the topic

Order/Paragraphs   No clear beginning or end

Voice   Some feelings shown

Word Choice   Repeated, dull words (*peple, good, evryone*); some incorrect words (*you hart and nees; you ear; a ear ake*)

Sentences   Too many ideas in some sentences

Rules   Many spelling mistakes (*docter, taks, peple, evryone, you, hart, nees, ake, Finely*); mistakes with capital letters and a contraction

© Pearson Education

Expository Writing Model *Score 1*

> The job im tell about is pilit. He takes you in a plan and you could go from new york to arzona Me and my dad went on a plan to florda? went to see dolfins at a sea park. The pilit took us bak home to.

Focus/Ideas   Ideas mixed up; ideas not on the topic; few facts

Order/Paragraphs   Paragraph not indented; no ending

Voice   Writer's feelings not shown

Word Choice   Dull; few words used to tell about job

Sentences   Should rewrite second sentence as three sentences

Rules   Many spelling mistakes *(im, pilit, plan, arzona, florda, dolfins, bak, to)*; mistakes with capital letters *(im, new york, arzona, florda)*; wrong words *(tell; Me and my dad)*; missing or wrong end punctuation; incomplete sentence

© Pearson Education

Check Your Writing

Check your writing by reading it over carefully. Try the following strategies.

Read your work aloud.

- If it sounds choppy, combine short sentences.

- Rewrite a long, stringy sentence as several sentences.

- Sentences should not all begin with *the* or *I*.

- Do ideas seem connected? If not, add words such as *then*, *next*, or *but*.

Check your style. It should match your audience and purpose.   You might begin an e-mail to a friend, "Hey, you won't believe the cool thing that happened." For a test, the following would be a better beginning: "An unusual thing happened today."

Be sure you have answered the prompt.

- Look for key words in the writing prompt.

  Compare a bike and a car. Tell two ways they are alike and two ways they are different.
  Topic: bike and car
  What you need to do: Compare
  What to include: Two likenesses and two differences

Make sure your writing is focused.   Take out sentences that are off the subject.

© Pearson Education

Check that there is enough support.

- Use details to give readers pictures.

- Support your opinion with reasons.

- Explain a main idea with good details.

Do you have a strong beginning? Does a question, a surprising fact, or an interesting detail get a reader's interest?

Is your ending good? A conclusion may say the main idea in a new way, tell what you have learned, or ask a question.

Check that you have used good words—and not too many of them.

- Strong verbs, precise nouns, and vivid adjectives make your writing clear and lively.

- Replace wordy phrases such as *blue in color* with *blue* and *in a careful way* with *carefully*.

© Pearson Education

Check List

- ☐ My writing sounds smooth and easy to read.

- ☐ I have used a good style for my audience and purpose.

- ☐ My writing answers the prompt or assignment.

- ☐ My writing is focused.

- ☐ I have used enough support.

- ☐ I have a strong beginning.

- ☐ I have a satisfying conclusion.

- ☐ I have used good words and avoided wordiness.

© Pearson Education

Grammar and Writing Lessons

Sentences

A **sentence** is a group of words that tells a complete idea. It begins with a capital letter. Many sentences end with a **period (.)**.

Pam has a cat. ⟵ This is a sentence.
Jack the cat ⟵ This is not a sentence.

A **Find** the sentence. **Underline** the sentence.

1. Jack the cat ran.

The cat

2. for Jack

I look for Jack.

3. The cat is in a sack.

is in a sack

4. Pam and I got the cat.

Pam and I

5. on my lap

Jack sat on my lap.

© Pearson Education

B **Find** the sentence. **Write** the sentence.

1. Don saw a pig.   saw a pig

_____

- -

_____

2. The pig   The pig is big.

_____

- -

_____

3. in a pen   The pig is in a pen.

_____

- -

_____

C **Choose** an animal. **Write** a sentence about it. **Use** a word from the box in your sentence.

| runs | swims | sits | plays |

_____

4. -

_____

_____

© Pearson Education

Test Preparation

 Mark the sentence.

1. ○ Pam saw a tiger today.
   ○ a tiger today
   ○ saw a tiger

2. ○ a tiger
   ○ A tiger is a big cat.
   ○ a big cat

3. ○ the tiger
   ○ will watch
   ○ She will watch the tiger.

4. ○ runs to
   ○ to the tree
   ○ The tiger runs to the tree.

5. ○ at Pam
   ○ The tiger looks at Pam.
   ○ The tiger looks at

© Pearson Education

Review

© Pearson Education

 Find the sentence. **Underline** the sentence.

1. has a pet dog

Dan has a pet dog.

2. The dog wants to play.

to play

3. The dog plays with the ball.

with the ball

 Finish each sentence. **Use** a group of words from the box. **Write** the sentence.

see a fox.	A fox	and see

4. I _____

in a box	lives in a box.	One cat

5. The cat _____

_____

_____

 **WRITER'S CRAFT**

Voice

> **Voice** is the <u>you</u> in your writing. It shows how you feel.
>
> **Weak Voice** I wore a blue shirt.
>
> **Strong Voice** This blue shirt makes me feel good.

Underline the sentence in each pair that tells how the writer feels.

1. I ate a pancake.

Warm pancakes are great.

2. Nora tells stories.

Nora is my best friend.

3. I have a new kitten.

I love this cute kitten.

4. I like scary books.

I read a book last week.

Write a sentence about your favorite kind of book. **Use** words that show how you feel.

_____

_____

_____

_____

_____

© Pearson Education

Tell About *You*

> **Writing Prompt**   Draw a picture to show what you and your friends like to do. Then write a sentence about the picture.

Writer tells what she likes to do and names her friends.

Drawing shows good details.

This is a complete sentence with a capital letter and a period.

I like to walk my dog with Becky and Lola.

© Pearson Education

Naming Parts of Sentences

A sentence has a **naming part.** It names a person, place, animal, or thing. The naming part tells who or what the sentence is about.

Max has a pig.   **The pig** has fun.

↑   ↑

naming part   naming part

A **Read** the sentence. **Circle** the naming part.

1. A wig is on the pig.

2. My hat is on the wig.

3. Max takes the hat.

4. Pam takes the wig.

5. The pig is sad.

© Pearson Education

B **Read** the sentence. **Write** the naming part.

1. One duck swims in the park.

_____

2. The park has a pond.

_____

3. Pat watches the duck.

_____

C **Complete** each sentence. **Write** a naming part.

4. _____ is my best toy.

5. _____ is my best friend.

6. _____ is the best month.

© Pearson Education

Test Preparation

☑ **Mark** the sentence that has a line under the naming part.

1. ○ The cat <u>is</u> big and black.
   ○ <u>The cat</u> is big and black.
   ○ The cat is <u>big and black</u>.

2. ○ <u>One pig</u> sits in the mud.
   ○ One pig <u>sits</u> in the mud.
   ○ One pig sits <u>in the mud</u>.

3. ○ That fox lives <u>in the woods</u>.
   ○ That fox <u>lives</u> in the woods.
   ○ <u>That fox</u> lives in the woods.

4. ○ <u>Two dogs</u> sat by the house.
   ○ Two dogs sat <u>by the house</u>.
   ○ Two dogs <u>sat</u> by the house.

5. ○ My bird <u>sits</u> in a cage.
   ○ My bird sits <u>in a cage</u>.
   ○ <u>My bird</u> sits in a cage.

© Pearson Education

Review

✅ **Circle** the naming part of each sentence.

1. Pat went to the pet shop.

2. The shop had many cats and dogs.

3. A dog licked Pat's hand.

✅ **Look** at each picture. **Write** the naming part of each sentence.

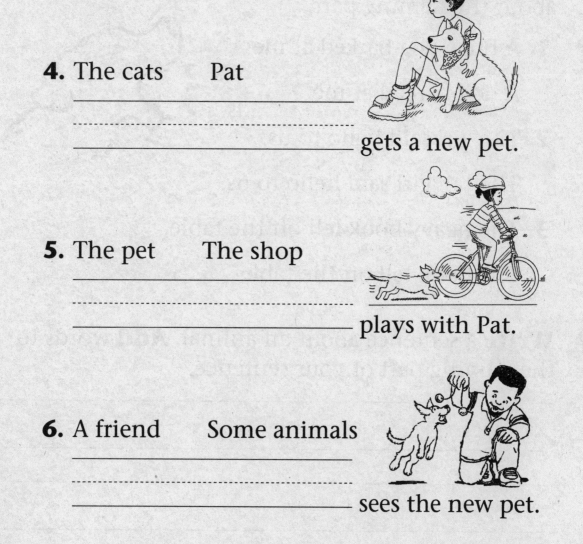

4. The cats   Pat

_____

- - - - - - - - - - -

_____ gets a new pet.

5. The pet   The shop

_____

- - - - - - - - - - -

_____ plays with Pat.

6. A friend   Some animals

_____

- - - - - - - - - - -

_____ sees the new pet.

© Pearson Education

Add Words to Naming Parts

Tell more about the **naming parts** of your sentences. **Add words** to give readers a clear picture.

No   A car stopped outside.

Yes   A <u>small</u>, <u>red</u> car stopped outside.

Circle the sentence in each pair that tells more about the naming part.

1. A huge dog barked at me.

A dog barked at me.

2. The girl said hello to us.

The tall girl said hello to us.

3. The heavy book fell off the table.

The book fell off the table.

Write a sentence about an animal. **Add** words to the naming part of your sentence.

_____

_____

_____

_____

© Pearson Education

Write a Caption

Writing Prompt Write a caption about this picture. Tell what is happening.

This is a complete sentence with a capital letter and a period.

Word tells about the cat.

The hungry cat wants to eat the fish.

Caption tells what is happening in the picture.

© Pearson Education

Action Parts of Sentences

A sentence has an **action part**. It tells what a person or thing does.

Mom and I **feed our pets.**   The dog **eats.**

↑   ↑

action part   action part

A **Read** the sentence. **Circle** the action part.

1. My dog barks.

2. The cat plays with a ball.

3. Her bird sings a song.

4. The horse runs.

5. One fish looks at me.

© Pearson Education

B **Read** the sentence. **Write** the action part.

1. The pig jumps in mud.

_____

- -

_____

2. The cat licks its paw.

_____

- -

_____

3. Nan rides a horse.

_____

- -

_____

C **Complete** each sentence. **Write** an action part.
Tell what the animal does.

_____

- -

4. A cow _____ .

_____

- -

5. A frog _____ .

_____

- -

6. A hen _____ .

© Pearson Education

Test Preparation

✓ **Mark** the sentence that has a line under the action part.

1. ○ <u>The goat</u> eats grass.
    ○ The <u>goat</u> eats grass.
    ○ The goat <u>eats grass</u>.

2. ○ Jan pets the <u>dog</u>.
    ○ Jan <u>pets the dog</u>.
    ○ <u>Jan</u> pets the dog.

3. ○ The cat <u>runs fast</u>.
    ○ The <u>cat</u> runs fast.
    ○ <u>The cat</u> runs fast.

4. ○ Her bird sings a <u>song</u>.
    ○ <u>Her bird</u> sings a song.
    ○ Her bird <u>sings a song</u>.

5. ○ <u>The hen</u> makes a nest.
    ○ The hen <u>makes a nest</u>.
    ○ The <u>hen</u> makes a nest.

© Pearson Education

Review

✓ **Circle** the action part of each sentence.

1. Pam pets the pig.

2. Rob tosses the ball.

3. Dad feeds the goat.

✓ **Look** at each picture. **Write** the action part of each sentence.

sleeps   flies

4. The bear _____ .

runs   swims

5. The fox _____ .

hops   eats

6. The frog _____ .

© Pearson Education

Tell What Happens

Tell more in the action parts of your sentences.
Add words to **tell what happens.**

No I pet the rabbit. Rabbits eat.

Yes I pet the <u>soft</u> rabbit. Rabbits eat <u>grass</u>.

Underline the sentence in each pair that tells
more about what happens.

1. The frog hops.

The frog hops into the pond.

2. She saw a bright yellow bird.

She saw a bird.

3. We helped the vet.

We helped.

Write a sentence about a job you do at home.
Add words to the action part of your sentence.

_____

_____

_____

© Pearson Education

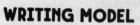

Tell About Helping Someone

Writing Prompt Write about a time when you helped someone. Draw a picture to show what you did.

I helped Mr. Ruiz rake leaves next door.

Writer tells how he helped and where.

This is a complete sentence with a capital letter and a period.

Drawing shows good details.

© Pearson Education

Word Order

The **order** of words in a sentence must make sense.

A den is in the fox.   ⟵   These words are not in the right order.

The fox is in a den.   ⟵   These words are in the right order.

Ⓐ Underline the words that are in the right order.

1. The fox has three kits.

Three fox the has kits.

2. A cave lives in the bear.

A bear lives in the cave.

3. Sleeps winter in the bear.

The bear sleeps in winter.

4. Woods in the deer the is.

The deer is in the woods.

5. Deer eat leaves on trees.

Trees on leaves eat deer.

© Pearson Education

B **Write** the words that are in the right order.

1. He pets a dog.   Pets he dog a.

_____

_____

_____

2. She feeds the hen.   The feeds she hen.

_____

_____

_____

3. The happy jumps boy.   The happy boy jumps.

_____

_____

_____

C **Finish** each sentence so that it makes sense.
Use words from the box.

| nap | bike | Reggie | Karen |

_____   _____

4. _____ rides the _____.

_____   _____

5. _____ takes a _____.

© Pearson Education

Test Preparation

✓ **Mark** the group of words that is in the correct order.

1. ○ Man the feeds a cow.
   ○ A man feeds the cow.
   ○ Cow a man feeds the.

2. ○ She pets a sheep.
   ○ A sheep pets she.
   ○ Pets she sheep a.

3. ○ Fox a runs away.
   ○ Away runs fox a.
   ○ A fox runs away.

4. ○ A cat play and dog a.
   ○ A cat and a dog play.
   ○ A play cat and a dog.

5. ○ The cat sleeps.
   ○ Sleeps the cat.
   ○ Cat the sleeps.

© Pearson Education

Review

 Underline the words that are in the right order.

1. Sam sees a lion.
A lion Sam sees.

2. The tiger sleeps.
Sleeps tiger the.

3. Ape hides the.
The ape hides.

 Write the words so they are in the right order. **End** each sentence with a period.

4. The plays ball seal.

_____

_____

5. Ball he likes the.

_____

_____

6. The ball seal the drops.

_____

_____

_____

© Pearson Education

Give Word Pictures

Your sentences should **give word pictures** to readers.

No I moved.

Yes I jumped over the fence.

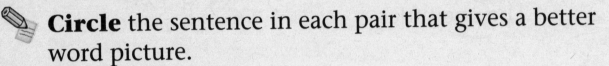 **Circle** the sentence in each pair that gives a better word picture.

1. It made noises.

The dog barked.

2. The glass smashed into pieces.

The glass fell.

3. He ran.

The boy rushed out the door.

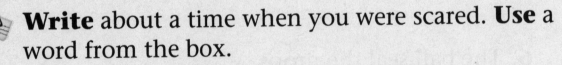 **Write** about a time when you were scared. **Use** a word from the box.

dark	ran	yelled

_____

_____

_____

_____

© Pearson Education

Tell About an Animal

Writing Prompt Tell about an animal you like. What does the animal look like and do?

Writer tells what monkeys do and look like.

Words give good details about the monkeys.

Description helps readers see the monkeys.

Funny Monkeys

Monkeys swing on trees.

They are brown and furry.

They make funny faces at me.

© Pearson Education

Telling Sentences

A **telling sentence** tells something. It is a statement. It begins with a **capital letter.** It usually ends with a **period (.)**.

The bird has one egg.
The egg is in the nest.

A **Put** a ✓ by the sentence that is right.

1. The nest is in the tree.   ——

the nest is in the tree   ——

2. we can see the nest   ——

We can see the nest.   ——

3. The bird sits on the egg.   ——

the bird sits on the egg   ——

4. the baby bird comes out   ——

The baby bird comes out.   ——

© Pearson Education

B **Find** the sentence. **Write** the sentence.

1. the rabbit hops   The rabbit hops.

_____

- -

_____

2. he sees the rabbit   He sees the rabbit.

_____

- -

_____

3. Rabbits eat carrots.   Rabbits eat carrots

_____

- -

_____

C **Write** two sentences about animals.
Begin and **end** each sentence correctly.

rabbit   bird   deer

- -

4. _____

_____

- -

5. _____

© Pearson Education

Test Preparation

✓ **Find** the sentence. **Mark** the sentence.

1. ○ the cow is black and white.
   ○ the cow is black and white
   ○ The cow is black and white.

2. ○ The cow lives in a barn
   ○ The cow lives in a barn.
   ○ the cow lives in a barn

3. ○ It eats grass.
   ○ it eats grass.
   ○ it eats grass

4. ○ Cows live with hens.
   ○ cows live with hens.
   ○ Cows live with hens

5. ○ A hen lays eggs
   ○ a hen lays eggs.
   ○ A hen lays eggs.

© Pearson Education

Review

 Put a ✓ by the sentence that is correct.

1. The girl feeds the dog. ___

   the girl feeds the dog ___

2. She pets the dog. ___

   she pets the dog ___

3. the dog runs with Nan ___

   The dog runs with Nan. ___

 Write each sentence correctly.

4. the hen has chicks

   _____
   -
   _____

5. the chicks are small

   _____
   -
   _____

6. Chicks stay in the nest

   _____
   -
   _____

© Pearson Education

Words That Tell How You Feel

Good writers tell how they feel. They use **words that show their feelings.**

Write a word from the box to tell how the writer feels.

| happy |
| sad |
| mad |

1. My sister broke my toy.

_____

I feel _____.

2. My best friend is here.

_____

I feel _____.

3. My cat is lost.

_____

I feel _____.

Write about a time when you were happy or sad. **Tell** how you felt.

_____

_____

_____

_____

_____

_____

© Pearson Education

Tell a Story

Writing Prompt   Tell a story about a real or a pretend pet. Tell something that happens to the pet.

Writer tells what
happens to a pet.

Readers learn
about the
writer's feelings.

Story has
an ending.

The Bird and the Cat

Once we had a cat and a bird. The bird flew out of its cage. Fritz got it. That made me sad. Now we just have a cat.

© Pearson Education

Questions

A **question** is an asking sentence. It begins with a **capital letter**. It ends with a **question mark (?)**.

Where are the animals?
Do you see the animals?

A **Underline** each question.

1. We see the zebra.

Can you see the zebra?

2. Where are the hippos?

Hippos hide in the water.

3. The lions are sleeping.

Are the lions sleeping?

4. Can elephants swim?

Elephants can swim.

80 Grammar

© Pearson Education

B **Find** the question. **Write** the question.

1. What is in the tree?   Birds are in the tree.

   _____

   -

   _____

2. Are tigers big?   Tigers are big.

   _____

   -

   _____

3. Dogs can bark.   Can dogs bark?

   _____

   -

   _____

C **Finish** the question. **Write** an animal name.

an ape   a giraffe   a seal

     _____

     - - - - - - - - - - - - - - - - -

What does _____ look like?

Answer the question. **Write** a sentence.

_____

- -

_____

© Pearson Education

Test Preparation

✓ **Find** the question. **Mark** the question.

1. ○ is that bird big?
   ○ Is that bird big?
   ○ That bird is big.

2. ○ Can you see the ostrich?
   ○ Can you see the ostrich
   ○ You can see the ostrich.

3. ○ Where is the bluebird
   ○ The bluebird is here.
   ○ Where is the bluebird?

4. ○ Is the hen white?
   ○ is the hen white
   ○ The hen is white.

5. ○ can the duck fly?
   ○ The duck can fly.
   ○ Can the duck fly?

© Pearson Education

Review

✓ **Write** each question. **Begin** and **end** the question correctly.

1. do you see a lion

_____

- - - - - - - - - - - - - - - - -

_____

2. does the lion roar

_____

- - - - - - - - - - - - - - - - -

_____

3. can the lion run

_____

- - - - - - - - - - - - - - - - -

_____

✓ **Look** at the words. **Put** them in order to write a question. **Begin** and **end** each question correctly.

4. can a bear swim

_____

- - - - - - - - - - - - - - - - -

_____

5. big the is bear

_____

- - - - - - - - - - - - - - - - -

_____

© Pearson Education

WRITER'S CRAFT

Ask Questions

Ask a question to start your writing.
Then answer the question.

Question   What do I want to be?

Answer   I want to be a chef. I love
                to cook. I will make many
                new dishes.

Finish the question below with a word from the box.

color	game	animal	food

What is my favorite _____?

Write an answer to the question above.

_____

_____

_____

_____

© Pearson Education

Answer a Question

Writing Prompt Think of an interesting animal. Write a question you would like to ask that animal. Write an answer that the animal might give.

Writer has written a question and an answer.

Writer uses a good word to show what the giraffe does.

Each sentence ends with the correct mark.

Mr. Giraffe

Why do you have that long neck, Mr. Giraffe?

I can nibble leaves in tall trees.

© Pearson Education

Nouns

A **noun** names a person, a place, an animal, or a thing.

The word **boy** names a person.

The word **rabbit** names an animal.

The word **pond** names a place.

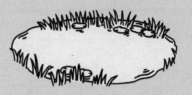

The word **pan** names a thing.

Ⓐ **Circle** the noun for each picture.

1.

school   park

2.

cat   dog

3.

man   girl

4.

bus   car

© Pearson Education

B **Write** the noun for each picture.

Person

girl   man

1. _____

Animal

cat   bird

3. _____

Place

park   zoo

2. _____

Thing

rug   cup

4. _____

C **Write** two sentences about your birthday.
Use some nouns from the box.

mom	dad	cake
grandma	grandpa	gift

_____

_____

_____

_____

© Pearson Education

Test Preparation

 Mark the noun that completes each sentence.

1. I set the ___.

- ○ table
- ○ clean
- ○ too

2. I have a little ___.

- ○ run
- ○ fish
- ○ the

3. We read ___.

- ○ books
- ○ long
- ○ tall

4. We wash ___.

- ○ all
- ○ up
- ○ dishes

5. I talk to my ___.

- ○ left
- ○ say
- ○ friend

© Pearson Education

Review

✓ **Circle** the noun in each sentence.

    1. Clean the house.

    2. Play with a ball.

    3. Walk the dog.

    4. Make the bed.

    5. Cut the grass.

✓ **Finish** each sentence.
Write a noun from the box.

sister	flowers	dad

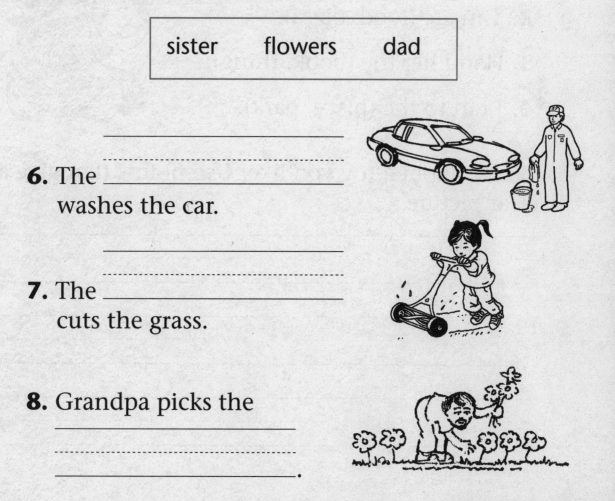

6. The _____
washes the car.

7. The _____
cuts the grass.

8. Grandpa picks the
_____
_____.

© Pearson Education

Use Nouns to Describe

Give readers clear pictures. **Use nouns to describe** things.

No I see a <u>bird</u>.

Yes I see a <u>robin</u>.

Circle the noun in ( ) that gives the reader a better picture.

1. Look at that (monkey, animal)!

2. Tim ate (food, pizza).

3. Hand her the (book, thing).

4. I ran to the (place, park).

Write about a toy you like. **Use** nouns that give a clear picture.

_____

- -

_____

- -

_____

- -

_____

© Pearson Education

Write a List

> **Writing Prompt** Write a list of things you do to help at home.

List shows things the writer does to help.

Nouns make the writing clear.

These sentences tell the order things are done.

I Help Dad

I help my dad fix things.

I open his toolbox.

I hand him the screwdriver.

I help him clean up when he is done.

© Pearson Education

Proper Nouns

Special names for people, places, animals, and things are called **proper nouns**. Proper nouns begin with capital letters.

 **M**ax   **O**ak **P**ark   **M**uffy   **B**ell **B**ridge

A **Look** at each picture.
Write the proper noun on the line.

Sam   **1.** This boy is _____.

North School   **2.** Sam goes to _____.

Elm Street   **3.** The school is on _____.

Smith Tower   **4.** It is near _____.

© Pearson Education

B **Correct** each name. **Write** it on the line.

1. beth

_____

- - - - - - - - - - - - - -

_____

3. lee school

_____

- - - - - - - - - - - - - -

_____

2. windy

_____

- - - - - - - - - - - - - -

_____

4. bay bridge

_____

- - - - - - - - - - - - - -

_____

C **Finish** each sentence with a proper noun.

_____

5. I live in _____.

(name of your city or town)

_____

6. My street is _____.

(name of your street)

© Pearson Education

Test Preparation

✓ **Mark** the sentence that is correct.

1. ○ This girl is Pat.
   ○ This girl is pat.
   ○ This girl is PAT.

2. ○ She lives near monk Park.
   ○ She lives near Monk Park.
   ○ She lives near monk park.

3. ○ This is oak school.
   ○ This is Oak school.
   ○ This is Oak School.

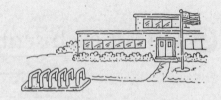

4. ○ The class pet is Ruby.
   ○ The class pet is ruby.
   ○ The class pet is RUBY.

5. ○ The class visits new york.
   ○ The class visits New York.
   ○ The class visits New YORK.

© Pearson Education

Review

 Circle the proper noun in each pair.

1. zoo   Parker Zoo

2. Emma   girl

3. Tim Tiger   cat

4. pond   Tuck Pond

Write the sentences.
Use a capital letter for each proper noun.

5. We are on west street.

_____

_____

6. Does tom live here?

_____

_____

7. There is hall park.

_____

_____

8. Does rex run there?

_____

_____

© Pearson Education

Use Proper Nouns in Writing

Use proper nouns. They tell readers more.

<u>The girl</u> played in <u>the park</u>.

↓ ↓

<u>Katie</u> played in <u>Oster Park</u>.

Circle the words in ( ) that tell readers more.

1. We visited (a city, Los Angeles).

2. The boys like (Coach Davis, the man).

3. I rode on (that horse, Bluebell).

4. They live on (Shell Place, a street).

Write about two friends and their pets.
Use their names.

_____

_____

_____

_____

_____

_____

© Pearson Education

Give Directions

> **Writing prompt**   Give directions about how to get from your home to a place nearby.

Directions are clear.

Proper nouns begin with capital letters.

Sentences are complete.

How to Get to James Park

Go out our door. Walk one block down Spruce Street to Oak Street. Turn right on Oak Street. Walk one block. You will see James Park.

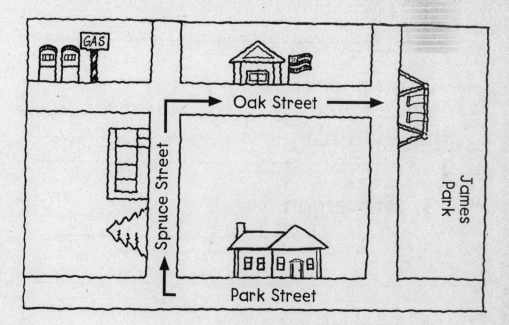

© Pearson Education

Special Titles

A **title** can come before the name of a person. A title begins with a **capital letter.** Some titles end with a **period (.).**

Captain Jones

Ms. Wong

Dr. Gold

A **Write** the title and the name correctly.

1. officer ruiz

2. mr popek

3. mrs vernon

4. miss falco

© Pearson Education

B **Match** each title and name to a picture.
Write the title and the name correctly.

| ms hunter | mr cortez | captain weber |

1. _____

2. _____

3. _____

C **Complete** the sentences. **Use** titles and names.

4. My teacher is _____.

5. My principal is _____.

6. My doctor is _____.

© Pearson Education

Test Preparation

☑ **Mark** the sentence that is correct.

1. ○ chief garcia fights fires.
   ○ Chief garcia fights fires.
   ○ Chief Garcia fights fires.

2. ○ My uncle is general Moy.
   ○ My uncle is General Moy.
   ○ My uncle is General moy.

3. ○ Miss stein is our principal.
   ○ Miss Stein is our principal.
   ○ miss stein is our principal.

4. ○ My teacher is Mr. Wilkin.
   ○ My teacher is mr. Wilkin.
   ○ My teacher is MR wilkin.

5. ○ Mrs. manos helps us cross.
   ○ mrs Manos helps us cross.
   ○ Mrs. Manos helps us cross.

© Pearson Education

Review

 Write the title and the name correctly.

1. captain bennet

_____

- - - - - - - - - - - - - - - -

_____

2. dr ortega

_____

- - - - - - - - - - - - - - - -

_____

3. mrs burke

_____

- - - - - - - - - - - - - - - -

_____

 Write each sentence correctly.
Use capital letters for the titles and names.

4. Does mr lu bring mail?

_____

- - - - - - - - - - - - - - - -

_____

5. My doctor is dr wilson.

_____

- - - - - - - - - - - - - - - -

_____

6. Is officer park at work?

_____

- - - - - - - - - - - - - - - -

_____

© Pearson Education

Write with Nouns

Make clear pictures for your readers. Use exact **nouns** that tell more.

We painted the <u>room</u>.

↓

We painted the <u>kitchen</u>.

Circle the noun that tells more about each picture.

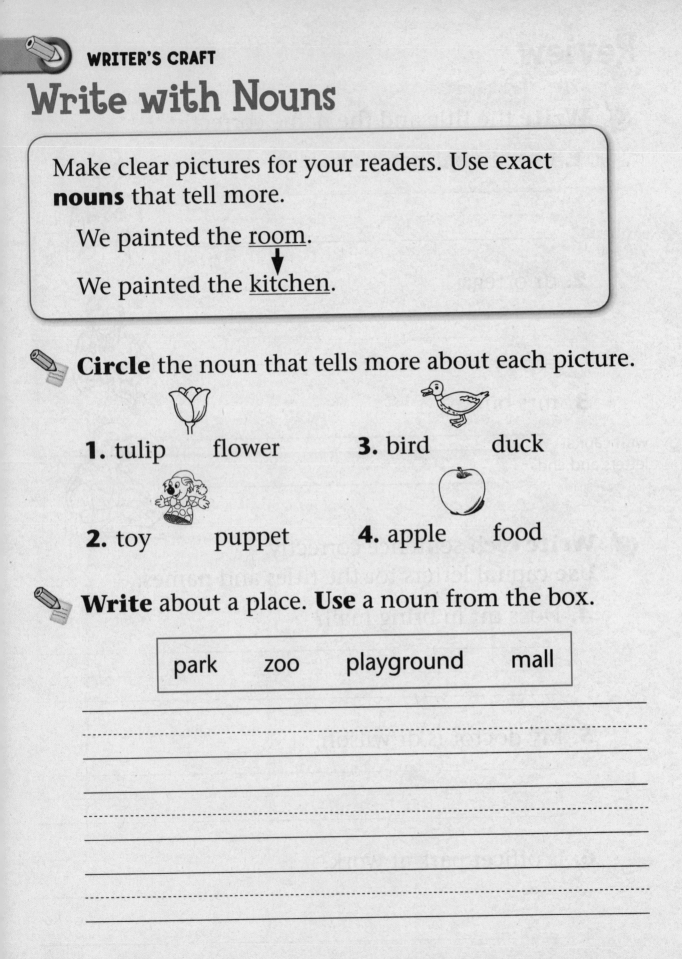

1. tulip   flower

3. bird   duck

2. toy   puppet

4. apple   food

Write about a place. **Use** a noun from the box.

park	zoo	playground	mall

_____

_____

_____

_____

_____

© Pearson Education

Write Rules

> **Writing Prompt** Write rules for owning a pet.

Writer has written clear rules for owning a pet.

Nouns give important information.

Sentences begin with capital letters and end with periods.

Rules for Pet Owners

Give your pet food and water.

Let your pet get exercise.

Keep your pet clean.

If your pet gets sick, take it to a vet.

Show your pet you care.

© Pearson Education

Days, Months, and Holidays

Days of the week begin with capital letters.

Sunday   Tuesday   Friday

Months of the year begin with capital letters.

January   April   September

Holidays begin with capital letters.

New Year's Day   Fourth of July

A **Write** the day, month, or holiday correctly.

1. On wednesday we had a class party.

_____

2. The weather is windy in march.

_____

3. We saw a parade on memorial day.

_____

4. This holiday is always on a monday.

_____

© Pearson Education

B **Write** each sentence. **Correct** the day, month, or holiday.

1. On tuesday Juan plays ball.

_____

- -

_____

2. In may Juan read two books.

_____

- -

_____

3. He will write a report before thanksgiving.

_____

- -

_____

C **Write** two sentences. **Use** two words in the box. **Write** the day, month, or holiday correctly.

| valentine's day | february | sunday |

_____

- -

_____

- -

_____

- -

_____

© Pearson Education

Test Preparation

✓ **Mark** the sentence that uses the day, month, or holiday correctly.

1. ○ In january I play in the snow.
   ○ In January I play in the snow.
   ○ In JanUary I play in the snow.

2. ○ On Friday we leave school early.
   ○ On friday we leave school early.
   ○ On FriDay we leave school early.

3. ○ We have a picnic on labor day.
   ○ We have a picnic on Labor Day.
   ○ We have a picnic on labor Day.

4. ○ Isn't Presidents' Day in winter?
   ○ Isn't Presidents' day in winter?
   ○ Isn't presidents' Day in winter?

5. ○ In july I swim in the pool.
   ○ In JULY I swim in the pool.
   ○ In July I swim in the pool.

© Pearson Education

Review

✓ **Write** the day, month, or holiday correctly.

1. Is there a holiday on wednesday?

_____

_____

2. Yes, it is veterans day.

_____

_____

3. That holiday is always in november.

_____

_____

✓ **Finish** the sentences. **Use** the words in the box. **Write** the day, month, or holiday correctly.

december	fourth of july	tuesday

4. Tomorrow is _____.

5. _____ is a cold month.

6. The _____ is fun.

© Pearson Education

Time-order Words

Use **time-order words** to show the order things happen. *First, next, then,* and *last* are time-order words.

<u>First</u> Sara walks to the bus stop. <u>Then</u> she waits for the bus. <u>Last</u> she gets on the bus.

Put the sentences in order. **Draw** a line from a time-order word to each sentence.

First   ___ the ant takes the food home.

Next   ___ an ant finds food.

Last   ___ the ant picks up the food.

Write about what you do in the morning after you get up. **Use** the words *first, next,* and *last.*

_____

_____

_____

_____

_____

_____

_____

_____

© Pearson Education

Write a Daily Plan

> **Writing Prompt**   Pick a day of the week. List four things you do on that day. Write the things you do in order. Use words such as *first*, *then*, *after*, and *last* to show time order.

A day of the week is spelled correctly.

Things the writer does are told in order.

After and *then* tell the order things are done.

Saturdays

On Saturday I go to soccer practice. After soccer Aunt Jill picks me up. Then we have lunch and walk her dog Scout. At four Dad comes to get me.

© Pearson Education

One and More Than One

Add **-s** to some nouns to mean more than one.

bug 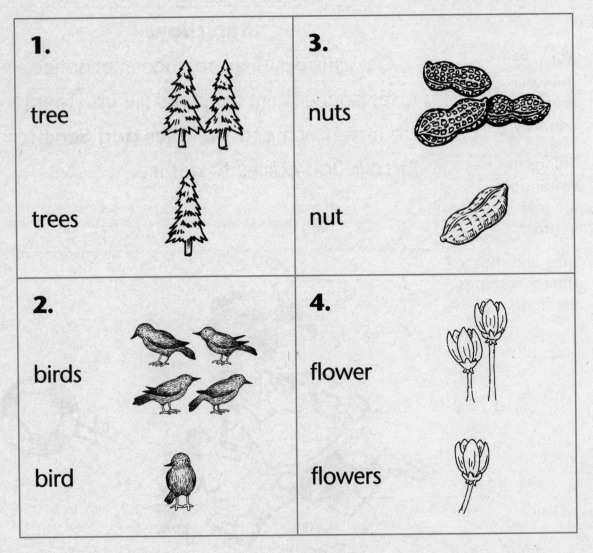   bug**s**

A **Draw** a line from the noun to the correct picture.

1.

tree

trees

2.

birds

bird

3.

nuts

nut

4.

flower

flowers

© Pearson Education

B **Write** the word in ( ) that is correct.

1. I see three (rock, rocks).

_____

- -

_____

2. One (rock, rocks) is white.

_____

- -

_____

3. Two (rabbit, rabbits) eat grass.

_____

- -

_____

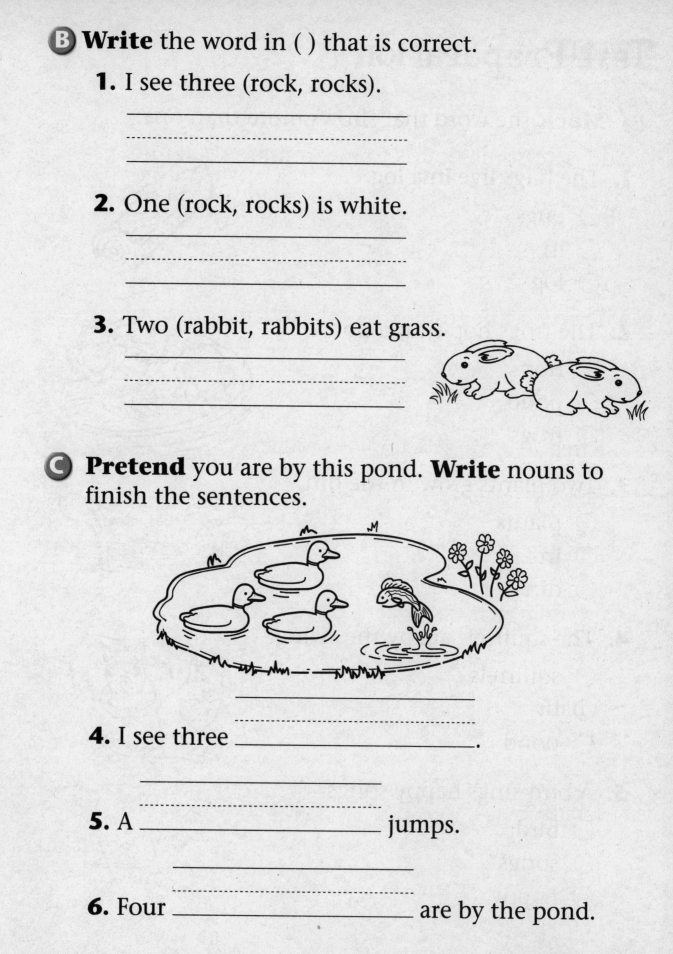

C **Pretend** you are by this pond. **Write** nouns to finish the sentences.

_____

- -

4. I see three _____.

_____

- -

5. A _____ jumps.

_____

- -

6. Four _____ are by the pond.

© Pearson Education

Test Preparation

 Mark the word that shows more than one.

1. The bugs live in a log.

○ bugs
○ in
○ log

2. The frogs hop near a pond.

○ hop
○ pond
○ frogs

3. Two plants grow in the dirt.

○ plants
○ in
○ dirt

4. The squirrels are by the swing.

○ squirrels
○ by
○ pond

5. A bird sings happy songs.

○ bird
○ songs
○ happy

© Pearson Education

Review

 Finish the sentences. **Write** the word in ( ) that is correct.

1. Four _____ grow.
   (flowers, flower)

2. One _____ eats.
   (cows, cow)

3. Two _____ sit.
   (bears, bear)

4. One _____ falls.
   (trees, tree)

5. Two _____ roll.
   (pigs, pig)

6. One _____ runs.
   (horses, horse)

© Pearson Education

Put Ideas in Order

Here is one way to **put ideas in order**. Tell what happens first, next, and last.

Lisa packs up her music book. She climbs on her bike. She rides to her piano lesson.

 Put these three sentences in the right order. **Write** *1*, *2*, or *3* in the box in front of each sentence.

☐ Clark puts the letter in the envelope.

☐ He takes the letter to the mailbox.

☐ Clark writes a letter to Amy.

Write about what could happen next.

_____

_____

_____

_____

_____

_____

© Pearson Education

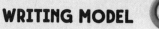

Describe a Special Place

Writing Prompt Tell about a special place outside. Tell why you like this place.

Writer tells why this place is special.

Correct words name one and more than one.

Sentences show the order things happen.

My Special Place

My special place is a tree in my uncle's yard. He nailed wooden blocks up the side. I use these as steps to climb the tree. Then I sit on the first branch. I feel like a king up there.

© Pearson Education

Nouns in Sentences

A **noun** names a person, a place, an animal, or a thing. A noun can be in more than one place in a sentence.

The **bees** have a **hive**.

A **Circle** the noun in each sentence. **Draw** and **color** a picture for each noun.

1. Look at the ant.

2. The tree is tall.

3. Where is the bird?

© Pearson Education

B **Circle** the two nouns in each sentence.

1. The hive is in a tree.

2. The bees help the queen.

3. The eggs are in cells.

4. The workers do a good job.

5. The boys like the honey.

C **Write** three sentences. **Tell** about kinds of bugs and where they live. **Use** some nouns from the box or your own nouns.

bees	ants	wasps
hives	hills	nests

_____

- - - - - - - - - - - - - - - - - - -

_____

- - - - - - - - - - - - - - - - - - -

_____

- - - - - - - - - - - - - - - - - - -

_____

- - - - - - - - - - - - - - - - - - -

_____

- - - - - - - - - - - - - - - - - - -

© Pearson Education

Test Preparation

 Mark the sentence that has a line under the noun.

1. ○ The ants <u>work</u> together.
   ○ The ants work <u>together</u>.
   ○ The <u>ants</u> work together.

2. ○ Look <u>at</u> the leaf.
   ○ Look at the <u>leaf</u>.
   ○ Look at <u>the</u> leaf.

3. ○ Where <u>is</u> the food?
   ○ <u>Where</u> is the food?
   ○ Where is the <u>food</u>?

4. ○ The <u>picnic</u> looks good.
   ○ The picnic looks <u>good</u>.
   ○ The picnic <u>looks</u> good.

5. ○ Other bugs come <u>too</u>.
   ○ Other <u>bugs</u> come too.
   ○ Other bugs <u>come</u> too.

© Pearson Education

Review

 Circle the two nouns in each sentence.

1. Ants are a team.

2. The nest is made of dirt.

3. A worker helps the queen.

4. These bugs build a hill.

5. Seeds may be their food.

 Finish the sentences. **Write** a noun from the box.

ants	Ann	yard

_____

6. _____ watches ants.

7. They live in her _____.

8. The _____ work hard.

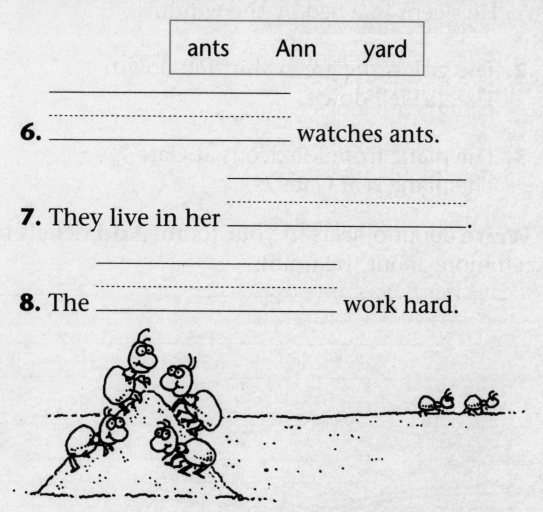

Add Details to Nouns

Tell more about nouns in your sentences. **Add details to nouns** to give readers a clear picture.

No   The boy is my friend.

Yes   The boy on the left is my friend.

Underline the sentence in each pair that tells more about the noun.

1. He sleeps in a bed.
He sleeps in a bed by the window.

2. The girl in the green shirt fell down.
The girl fell down.

3. The plane from Mexico is at Gate 7.
The plane is at Gate 7.

Write about objects in your room. **Add** details to tell more about the nouns.

_____

_____

_____

_____

_____

_____

© Pearson Education

Write Facts

Writing Prompt Write facts about an insect. How does it move? Where does it live? What does it do?

Writer gives good facts and details about bees.

Nouns give clear pictures.

Focus stays on bees.

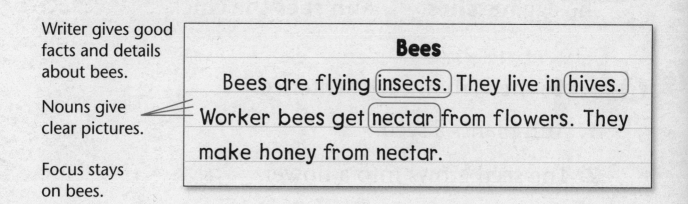

Bees

Bees are flying [insects.] They live in [hives.] Worker bees get [nectar] from flowers. They make honey from nectar.

© Pearson Education

Action Verbs

A **verb** tells what someone or something does.

The egg **hatches**.   Ann **sees** the chick.

A **Circle** the verb in each sentence.

1. Ann plants a seed.

2. The seed grows into a flower.

3. The sun rises in the morning.

4. The sun sets in the evening.

5. Snow falls on the ground.

6. The sun melts the snow.

7. The baby crawls on the floor.

8. The child runs to the door.

© Pearson Education

B **Write** the verb in each sentence.

_____

1. The sun shines.   _____

2. The flowers open.   _____

3. Ming picks the flowers.   _____

C **Write** three sentences about something that happens outdoors. **Use** action verbs from the box or your own words.

| grow   fall   bloom |

_____

_____

_____

_____

© Pearson Education

Test Preparation

✓ **Mark** the sentence that has a line under the verb.

1. ○ The <u>warm</u> sun rises.

   ○ The warm <u>sun</u> rises.

   ○ The warm sun <u>rises</u>.

2. ○ Jan <u>smiles</u> at it.

   ○ <u>Jan</u> smiles at it.

   ○ Jan smiles at <u>it</u>.

3. ○ Then <u>rain</u> clouds hide it.

   ○ Then rain <u>clouds</u> hide it.

   ○ Then rain clouds <u>hide</u> it.

4. ○ Jan <u>runs</u> inside.

   ○ Jan runs <u>inside</u>.

   ○ <u>Jan</u> runs inside.

5. ○ Soon the <u>rain</u> stops.

   ○ Soon the rain <u>stops</u>.

   ○ <u>Soon</u> the rain stops.

© Pearson Education

Review

 Circle the verb in each sentence.

1. Tom sees the fish.

2. The fish swims in the bowl.

3. Ned calls his father.

4. The child grabs the toy.

5. Ella washes the dishes.

 Circle the correct verb in ( ) to complete each sentence. **Write** the verb on the line.

6. The horse _____ in the field.
   (laughs, runs)

7. The girl _____ an apple.
   (eats, sleeps)

8. The man _____ a friend.
   (calls, shuts)

© Pearson Education

Strong Verbs

Use **strong verbs.** They show readers exactly what is happening.

Weak Verb   Laura <u>goes</u> to Carlos's house.

Strong Verb   Laura <u>races</u> to Carlos's house.

Look at the verbs in dark type. Which sentence has a stronger verb? **Circle** the sentence.

1. The baby **puts** his spoon on the floor.

The baby **throws** his spoon on the floor.

2. He **grabs** his bottle.

He **gets** his bottle.

3. He **goes** across the rug.

He **crawls** across the rug.

Write about an activity you do after school. **Use** strong verbs. **Show** readers what you are doing.

_____

_____

_____

© Pearson Education

Write a Song

Writing Prompt   Write a song about an animal. Use strong verbs. Tell what that animal does or looks like.

This Bird Peeps

[to the tune of "This Old Man"]

This bird peeps.

That bird peeps.

Did you know that each bird speaks?

They can chirp and chatter.

Listen while you walk.

We can hear the birdies talk.

Song uses strong verbs to tell what birds sound like.

Rhyme makes the song interesting.

Song focuses on the sounds of birds.

© Pearson Education

Writing   **127**

Verbs That Add -s

A **verb** can tell what one person, animal, or thing does. Add **-s** to show what is being done now.

Ruby **eats** a bug.   The duck **swims** in the lake.

A **Underline** the correct verb in ( ).

1. Danny (crawl, crawls) across the floor.

2. The girl (ride, rides) her bike.

3. The baby (make, makes) funny sounds.

4. Alice (tell, tells) a story.

5. Susie (nap, naps) in a crib.

6. The boy (sleep, sleeps) in a bed.

© Pearson Education

B Complete each sentence.
Write the correct verb on the line.

1. The man _____ a tune.

   (plays, play)

2. Kate _____ a pear.

   (eat, eats)

3. Tim _____ something.

   (hear, hears)

C Look at the picture. **Write** a verb to finish each sentence. **Remember** to add -s to each verb.

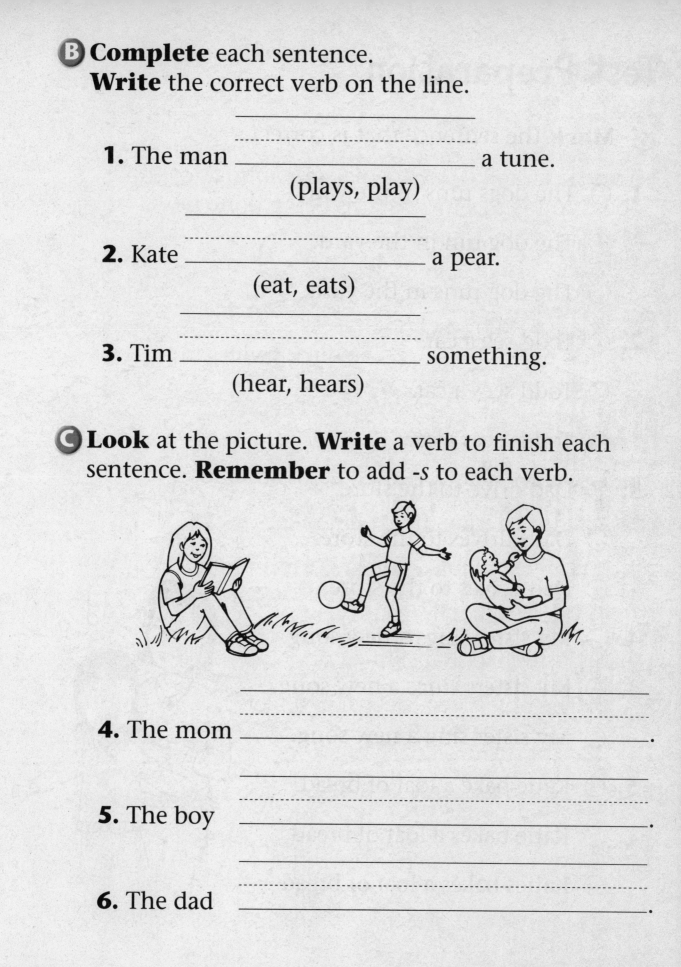

4. The mom _____.

5. The boy _____.

6. The dad _____.

© Pearson Education

Test Preparation

✓ **Mark** the sentence that is correct.

1. ○ The dogs runs in the yard.

   ○ The dog run in the yard.

   ○ The dog runs in the yard.

2. ○ Todd see a car.

   ○ Todd sees a car.

   ○ Todds sees a car.

3. ○ Dad drive to the store.

   ○ Dads drives to the store.

   ○ Dad drives to the store.

4. ○ My sister sings a new song.

   ○ My sisters sings a new song.

   ○ My sister sing a new song.

5. ○ Katie bake a loaf of bread.

   ○ Katie bakes a loaf of bread.

   ○ Katies bakes a loaf of bread.

© Pearson Education

Review

✓ **Complete** each sentence.
Underline the correct verb in ( ).

1. The cat (roll, rolls) in the grass.

2. The man (buys, buy) food.

3. The girl (bring, brings) a game.

4. Omar (call, calls) his friend.

5. Lucy (opens, open) the door.

✓ **Add** -s to the verb in ( ) to complete each sentence.
Write the verb on the line.

6. Kim _____ now. (sleep)

7. Pam _____ away. (crawl)

8. Max _____ milk. (drink)

© Pearson Education

Action Verbs

Use **action verbs** to show your readers
exactly what happens.

No   He <u>puts</u> a picture on the wall.
Yes   He <u>hangs</u> a picture on the wall.

Write the correct verb from the box to complete
each sentence.

eats	races	scoops

1. The dog _____ to the kitchen.

2. Tim _____ food into the dish.

3. The dog _____ the food.

Write about something you do. **Use** action verbs.

_____

_____

_____

_____

© Pearson Education

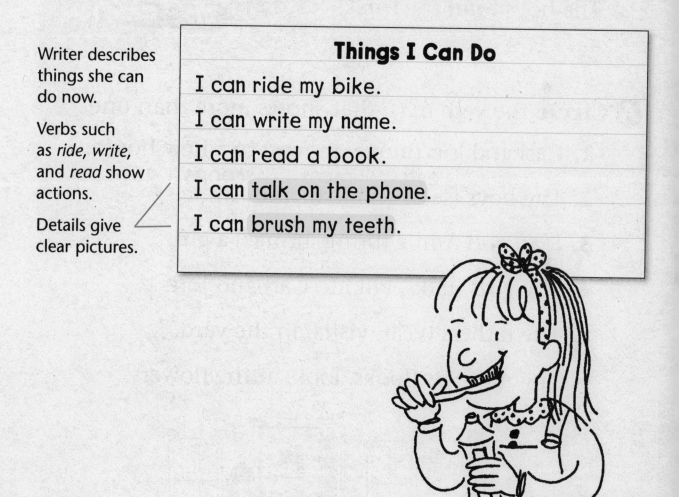

Tell What You Can Do

Writing Prompt Describe things you can do now that you could not do when you were a baby. Use action verbs.

Writer describes things she can do now.

Verbs such as *ride*, *write*, and *read* show actions.

Details give clear pictures.

Things I Can Do

I can ride my bike.

I can write my name.

I can read a book.

I can talk on the phone.

I can brush my teeth.

© Pearson Education

Verbs That Do Not Add -s

Do not add **-s** to a verb that tells what two or more people, animals, or things do now.

Mom and Dad **pack** boxes.

The boys **load** the truck.

A **Circle** the verb in ( ) that shows more than one.

1. Carl and Jon (move, moves) to a new house.

2. The boys (sees, see) Joan and Annie.

3. Joan and Annie (bring, brings) a gift.

4. The girls (talks, talk) to Carl and Jon.

5. The fathers (visit, visits) in the yard.

6. The mothers (looks, look) at the flowers.

© Pearson Education

B **Write** the verb in ( ) that shows more than one.

1. The boys (waits, wait) here. _____

2. Toys (sit, sits) in boxes. _____

3. Two men (take, takes) the boxes upstairs. _____

C **Choose** a verb from the box to complete each sentence. **Write** the verb.

laugh	own	splash

4. Three dogs _____ in the water.

5. Four girls _____ at them.

6. Ed and May _____ the dogs.

© Pearson Education

Test Preparation

✓ **Mark** the sentence that is correct.

1. ○ Mom and Dad buy a new house.
   ○ Mom and Dad buys a new house.
   ○ Mom buy a new house.

2. ○ Terry and Nick meets new friends.
   ○ Terry and Nick meet new friends.
   ○ Terry meet new friends.

3. ○ The friends lives on their street.
   ○ The friends live on their street.
   ○ The friend live on their street.

4. ○ The boys see their new school.
   ○ The boys sees their new school.
   ○ The boy see their new school.

5. ○ Their new teachers talks to them.
   ○ Their new teacher talk to them.
   ○ Their new teachers talk to them.

© Pearson Education

Review

✓ **Circle** the verb that shows more than one.

1. Nan and Mary (packs, pack) their toys.

2. Their parents (put, puts) tags on the boxes.

3. The men (loads, load) the boxes.

4. The cats (run, runs) into the yard.

5. Fluffy and Beano (hides, hide) there.

✓ **Circle** the correct verb.
Write the verb on the line.

6. The movers _____ the truck.
(drive, drives)

7. The girls _____ boxes.
(takes, take)

8. Two pets _____ out!
(jumps, jump)

© Pearson Education

WRITER'S CRAFT
Focus/Ideas

Good writers tell about one **idea.** Every sentence tells about that idea.

 Two sentences do NOT belong. **Draw** a line through the sentences.

1. The plane rolls down the runway.

It moves faster and faster.

Do you like planes?

The plane rises into the air.

I watch planes all the time.

Soon it is high in the sky.

Finish the sentence below. **Write** two other sentences about this idea.

I will go to _____

_____

_____

_____

© Pearson Education

Make a Greeting Card

Writing Prompt Write a greeting card. Welcome a new student named Jay to your school and class.

Hello, Jay

Card welcomes Jay.

Hello, Jay!

Welcome to Room 105.

Ms. Guthrie's class

Details focus on class activities.

Every morning we have Show and Tell. We named our gerbil Henry. You can help us finish our mural. It is called Facts about Florida.

Voice of the card is friendly.

The First Graders

© Pearson Education

Writing **139**

Verbs for Now and the Past

Verbs can tell what happens now. Verbs can tell what happened in the past. Some verbs that tell about the past end with **-ed.**

Frog **works.** (now)

Frog **worked.** (past)

A **Read** each word in the box. **Write** the word under *Now* if it tells about now. **Write** the word under *The Past* if it tells about the past.

| shouted | looks | talks | walked | shows | waited |

Now   **The Past**

1. _____   4. _____

2. _____   5. _____

3. _____   6. _____

© Pearson Education

B **Circle** the correct verb in ( ) to complete each sentence.

1. Last month Frog (plants, planted) some seeds.

2. Now Frog (plants, planted) more seeds.

3. Last week Frog (waters, watered) the plants.

4. Last year Frog (picks, picked) many flowers.

5. Now Frog (picks, picked) flowers again.

C **Finish** the sentences.
Use the correct form of the verb in ( ).

6. Last summer I _____ Grandma. (visit)

7. Now I _____ her every week. (call)

8. Yesterday we _____ for an hour. (talk)

© Pearson Education

Test Preparation

✓ **Mark** the sentence that is correct.

1. ○ Last month Jon plant a garden.
   ○ Last month Jon planted a garden.
   ○ Last month Jon plants a garden.

2. ○ Ted visits the garden now.
   ○ Ted visited the garden now.
   ○ Ted visit the garden now.

3. ○ Nan pick flowers yesterday.
   ○ Nan picks flowers yesterday.
   ○ Nan picked flowers yesterday.

4. ○ Today the garden look pretty.
   ○ Today the garden looked pretty.
   ○ Today the garden looks pretty.

5. ○ Last year the garden needed more sun.
   ○ Last year the garden need more sun.
   ○ Last year the garden needs more sun.

© Pearson Education

Review

☑ **Circle** the correct verb in ( ).

1. Last week Pam (walked, walks) in the park.

2. Now she (walked, walks) in the garden.

3. Ryan (calls, called) his friend yesterday.

4. Today Pam (calls, called) her friend.

☑ **Complete** each sentence. **Write** the correct verb on the line.

5. Last week Ed _____ for Mom.

(waits, waited)

6. Today he _____ in the yard.

(plays, play)

7. Last night Cam _____ to Dad.

(talked, talks)

8. Now she _____ her friend.

(visited, visits)

© Pearson Education

Rhyme

A writer may use two words with the same ending sounds. These words **rhyme**.

> Rain, rain, go <u>away</u>!
> Come again some other <u>day</u>!

Away and *day* have the same ending sounds.

 Circle the words that rhyme.

1. Snow falls down.
It gets all over.
It blows into piles.
It brings children smiles.

2. It's been raining for hours.
That's good for the flowers,
But not so good for me.
I want to play in the yard!

Write two sentences about your favorite weather.
Use at least two words that rhyme.

_____

_____

_____

_____

_____

_____

_____

© Pearson Education

Write a Poem

> **Writing Prompt** Write a poem about something that grows. Your topic could be seeds, flowers, trees—or you!

This is a lively poem about seeds growing.

Different kinds of sentences make the poem interesting.

Writer uses rhyming words.

Something Green

Seeds need water.

Seeds need sun.

Watch them growing.

This is fun!

Do you see a tiny sprout?

Something green is peeking out!

© Pearson Education

Am, Is, Are, Was, and Were

The words **am**, **is**, and **are** tell about now. Use **am** or **is** to tell about one. Use **are** to tell about more than one.

I **am** big.   It **is** small.   They **are** small.

The words **was** and **were** tell about the past. Use **was** to tell about one. Use **were** to tell about more than one.

It **was** hungry.   They **were** hungry.

A **Circle** the verb in each sentence. **Write** *Now* if the sentence tells about now. **Write** *Past* if the sentence tells about the past.

1. I am a butterfly. _____

2. I was a caterpillar. _____

3. Butterflies are on the flowers. _____

© Pearson Education

B **Circle** the correct verb in ( ) to complete the sentence.

1. These bugs (was, were) little.

2. Now one bug (is, are) big.

3. The boy and girl (is, are) happy.

4. I (am, are) happy too.

5. Yesterday (was, were) a good day.

C **Complete** each sentence. **Write** a verb from the box.

is

were

am

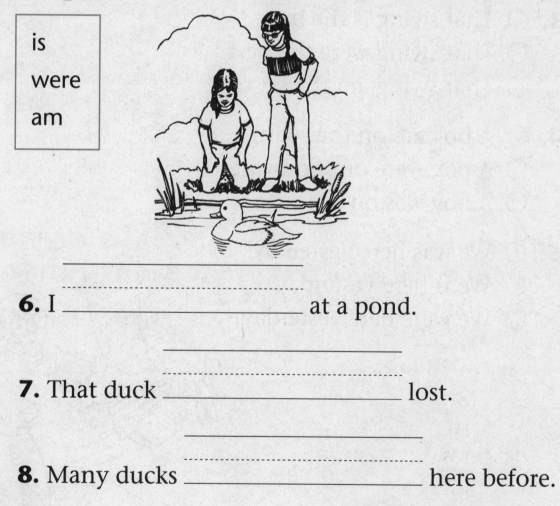

6. I _____ at a pond.

7. That duck _____ lost.

8. Many ducks _____ here before.

© Pearson Education

Test Preparation

✓ **Mark** the sentence that is correct.

1. ○ Kara and Sue are at the park.
   ○ Kara and Sue is at the park.
   ○ Kara and Sue was at the park.

2. ○ I are with the girls.
   ○ I am with the girls.
   ○ I is with the girls.

3. ○ That swing is the best.
   ○ That swing were the best.
   ○ That swing am the best.

4. ○ A boy are on the swing.
   ○ A boy were on the swing.
   ○ A boy was on the swing.

5. ○ We was here yesterday.
   ○ We is here yesterday.
   ○ We were here yesterday.

© Pearson Education

Review

 Circle the correct verb in ( ) to complete each sentence.

1. Yesterday I (am, was) in the garden.

2. The flowers (are, is) red and pink.

3. Two birds (was, were) nearby.

4. One bird (were, was) yellow.

5. Today it (is, were) on a red flower.

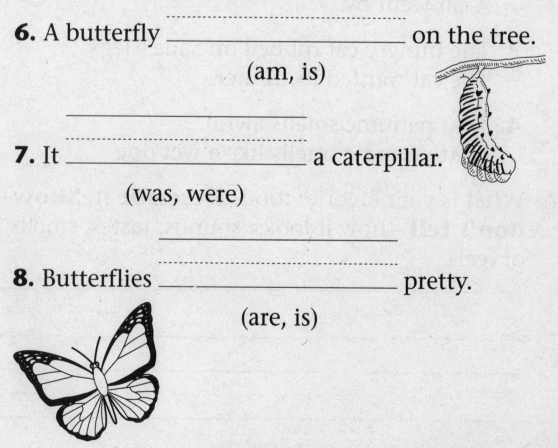 **Choose** the correct verb in ( ) to complete the sentence. **Write** the verb on the line.

6. A butterfly _____ on the tree.

(am, is)

7. It _____ a caterpillar.

(was, were)

8. Butterflies _____ pretty.

(are, is)

© Pearson Education

Show, Don't Tell

When you write about something, **show—don't tell**—how it looks, sounds, tastes, smells, or feels.

No   I drank hot chocolate.

Yes The hot chocolate burned my tongue.

Underline the sentence in each pair that shows rather than tells.

1. The flowers are pretty.
   Yellow poppies glow in the sun.

2. A car roared down the street.
   A car went by.

3. The hungry cat rubbed on Sada's legs.
   The cat wanted its dinner.

4. That perfume smells awful.
   That perfume smells like a wet dog.

What is your favorite food? **Describe** it. **Show—don't tell**—how it looks, sounds, tastes, smells, or feels.

_____

_____

_____

_____

© Pearson Education

Describe a Caterpillar

Writing Prompt   Describe a caterpillar. Tell about its color and how it moves. Tell how it feels crawling on your hand.

Writer shows how the caterpillar looks and feels.

Last sentence states a fact about the caterpillar.

Description stays focused on the caterpillar.

It Tickles

The caterpillar crawls on my hand. It tickles. It looks fuzzy and has brown and green stripes. Some day it will turn into a beautiful butterfly.

© Pearson Education

Contractions with *Not*

A **contraction** is a short way to put two words together. A **verb** and the word **not** can be put together to make a contraction. An **apostrophe (')** is used in place of the letter **o**.

are + not = aren't   has + not = hasn't

did + not = didn't   is + not = isn't

do + not = don't   was + not = wasn't

does + not = doesn't   were + not = weren't

A **Circle** the contraction in each sentence. **Draw** a line to the words for the contraction.

1. Bears aren't awake in winter.   do not

2. Some birds don't stay in the cold.   was not

3. The geese weren't gone yet.   are not

4. That squirrel isn't sleeping.   were not

5. The deer wasn't finding food.   is not

© Pearson Education

B **Write** the contraction for the underlined words.

1. A bear <u>does not</u> wake up all winter.

2. The squirrel <u>has not</u> built a nest.

3. The hummingbird <u>did not</u> wait for winter.

4. The geese <u>are not</u> flying south yet.

5. The butterfly <u>is not</u> coming out until spring.

C **Write** sentences about what happens in the winter. **Use** a contraction with *not* in each sentence.

6. Bears _____

7. The goose _____

8. That flower _____

© Pearson Education

Test Preparation

☑ **Mark** the sentence that spells the contraction correctly.

1. ○ It doesnt snow in summer.
   ○ It doesn't snow in summer.
   ○ It doesnt' snow in summer.

2. ○ The birds weren't here in winter.
   ○ The birds were'nt here in winter.
   ○ The birds werent here in winter.

3. ○ Squirrels dont stay in their nests.
   ○ Squirrels don't stay in their nests.
   ○ Squirrels do'nt stay in their nests.

4. ○ It hasnt snowed this winter.
   ○ It hasnt' snowed this winter.
   ○ It hasn't snowed this winter.

5. ○ The squirrel did'nt find the nut.
   ○ The squirrel didnt find the nut.
   ○ The squirrel didn't find the nut.

© Pearson Education

Review

 Draw a line from the words to their contraction.

1. has not   isn't

2. were not   aren't

3. did not   don't

4. was not   doesn't

5. are not   didn't

6. does not   weren't

7. is not   wasn't

8. do not   hasn't

Write the contraction for the underlined words.

9. Geese <u>do not</u> stay in winter. _____

10. A raccoon <u>does not</u> leave. _____

11. The butterfly <u>has not</u> come out. _____

12. Spring <u>is not</u> as cold as winter. _____

© Pearson Education

Main Idea Sentences

The **main idea** is what a paragraph is about. A sentence in the paragraph tells the main idea.

Circle the main idea sentence in each paragraph.

1. Animals come in many sizes. A spider is tiny, and a whale is huge. Turtles are short, and giraffes are tall. A bear is fat, and a snake is skinny.

2. Tina packed her lunch for school. She placed an apple and a ham and cheese sandwich in a bag. Then she dropped in some carrots and a granola bar.

Write a main idea sentence for the following paragraph.

_____ He can stand and walk on his back legs. He can catch a stick when you throw it. Otto can find things when you hide them. That dog can even turn flips in the air!

_____

_____

_____

© Pearson Education

Describe a Season

> **Writing Prompt** Describe a season. Write a main idea sentence and three supporting sentences about the season.

Writer begins with a main idea sentence about spring.

Other sentences support the main idea sentence.

Sentences have a smooth, pleasing style.

Spring

Spring is when everything wakes up.

Trees were asleep, but now they are green. Animals were hiding, but here comes a robin. Flowers were resting, but now tulips bloom.

© Pearson Education

Adjectives

An **adjective** tells about a person, place, animal, or thing.

small boy

big farm

brown cow

funny book

A **Circle** the adjective.

1. sharp pencil

2. white paper

3. tall man

4. new house

5. loud dog

6. bright sun

7. fluffy chick

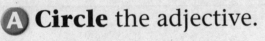

8. happy girl

© Pearson Education

B **Write** the adjective on the line.

1. She buys green pears. _____

2. He likes hard books. _____

3. They watch long movies. _____

C **Write** an adjective from the box to complete each sentence.

| yellow | huge | sweet |

4. He has a _____ pumpkin.

5. She eats a _____ banana.

6. I pick _____ berries.

© Pearson Education

Test Preparation

☑ **Mark** the sentence that has a line under the adjective.

1. ○ I read a sad <u>book</u>.
   ○ I read a <u>sad</u> book.
   ○ <u>I</u> read a sad book.

2. ○ <u>It</u> was about a brave dog.
   ○ It <u>was</u> about a brave dog.
   ○ It was about a <u>brave</u> dog.

3. ○ I had a <u>big</u> frown on my face.
   ○ I had a big frown on my <u>face</u>.
   ○ I had a big frown <u>on</u> my face.

4. ○ My <u>best</u> friend made me smile.
   ○ My best friend <u>made</u> me smile.
   ○ My best friend made <u>me</u> smile.

5. ○ <u>Mark</u> told me a funny joke.
   ○ Mark told me a <u>funny</u> joke.
   ○ Mark <u>told</u> me a funny joke.

© Pearson Education

Review

 Look at the picture.
Circle the correct adjective in ( ).

1. Pari has a (big, little) dog.

2. His dog has (white, black) fur.

3. Skip wags his (long, short) tail.

 Complete each sentence. **Write** an adjective from the box.

sharp	old	playful

4. José likes _____ dogs.

5. Dana wants _____ pencils.

6. I have _____ shoes.

© Pearson Education

Strong Adjectives

Strong adjectives can give readers clear pictures. Do not always use *nice, pretty,* or *good.* Use adjectives that tell more.

No   I sat in the nice garden.

Yes   I sat in the peaceful garden.

Circle the sentence with the adjective that tells more.

1. Ann drew a pretty picture.

Ann drew a colorful picture.

2. Mr. Ho wore a gray suit.

Mr. Ho wore a nice suit.

3. Butch is a good dog.

Butch is a frisky dog.

Write about a place you like. **Use** strong adjectives.

_____

_____

_____

_____

_____

_____

© Pearson Education

Write a Book Review

Writing Prompt   Tell about a book you like. Use adjectives to show readers what you like about the book.

Writer names the book in the first sentence.

Adjectives tell readers about the book.

Last sentence tries to persuade readers to read this book.

A Good Book

I like <u>The Cat in the Hat</u>. It is a funny story by Dr. Seuss. A strange cat visits two children. He makes a terrible mess. If you want to laugh, read this great book.

© Pearson Education

Adjectives for Colors and Shapes

Some **adjectives** name colors.

red apple   **black** dog

Some **adjectives** name shapes.

round rug 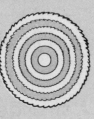 **square** frame

A **Underline** the adjective in each sentence that names a color or a shape.

1. Van draws on white paper.

2. He fills it with round dots.

3. He uses green markers.

4. Van makes square boxes too.

5. He adds yellow flowers.

6. He gives them oval leaves.

© Pearson Education

B **Write** the adjective in each sentence that names a color or shape.

1. Rosa cuts round circles. _____

2. Ken draws blue stars. _____

3. I paste them on red paper. _____

C **Color** the picture. **Write** about the picture. **Use** color and shape words.

_____

© Pearson Education

Test Preparation

☑ **Mark** the sentence that has a line under the adjective.

1. ○ She <u>painted</u> a blue house.
   ○ <u>She</u> painted a blue house.
   ○ She painted a <u>blue</u> house.

2. ○ It has square <u>windows</u>.
   ○ It has <u>square</u> windows.
   ○ <u>It</u> has square windows.

3. ○ Max draws with a <u>red</u> pencil.
   ○ Max draws <u>with</u> a red pencil.
   ○ <u>Max</u> draws with a red pencil.

4. ○ The ladybug is on a green <u>leaf</u>.
   ○ The ladybug is on a <u>green</u> leaf.
   ○ The <u>ladybug</u> is on a green leaf.

5. ○ The bug has <u>round</u> dots on its back.
   ○ The bug has round dots on its <u>back</u>.
   ○ The bug <u>has</u> round dots on its back.

© Pearson Education

Review

✓ **Underline** the adjective to make each sentence correct.

1. Omar has a (red, talk) marker.

2. He draws a (round, go) apple.

3. Abby has a (see, square) piece of paper.

4. She uses her (yellow, has) crayon.

✓ **Choose** the adjective in ( ). **Write** the adjective.

5. I get _____ paper.
   (blue, say)

6. Dad cuts out _____ cars.
   (help, square)

7. He cuts out _____ tires.
   (think, round)

8. I make _____ tires.
   (black, sleep)

© Pearson Education

WRITER'S CRAFT
Good Endings

A **good ending** wraps up your ideas. It lets readers know you are finished.

I missed the bus. My shoelace broke. I lost my lunchbox. My first day at school was awful.

Underline the best ending for the paragraph.

Navi played soccer on Tuesday and Thursday. On Wednesday she went to her violin lesson. She worked at the library on Friday.

A On Saturday Navi didn't have a plan.

B Navi had a busy week.

C Monday was a holiday.

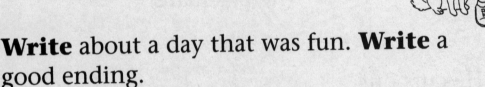

Write about a day that was fun. **Write** a good ending.

_____
_____
_____
_____
_____

© Pearson Education

Tell About a Color

Writing Prompt   Tell about your favorite color. Why do you like it? What things are this color?

Purple

Purple is my favorite color. My birthstone is purple. Grapes can be purple. I have three t-shirts that are purple. Can you guess why my shortest crayon is purple?

Writer tells what things are her favorite color.

Each sentence begins with a different word. This makes the paragraph interesting.

A question to the reader is a good ending.

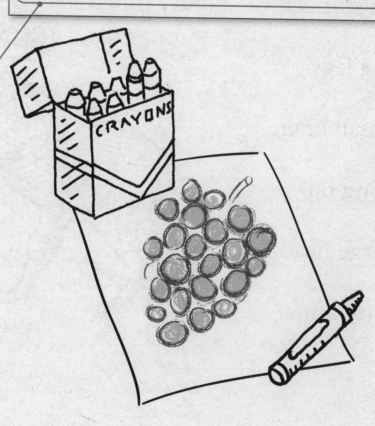

© Pearson Education

Adjectives for Sizes

Some **adjectives** describe size. Words such as *big*, *small*, *long*, and *short* describe size.

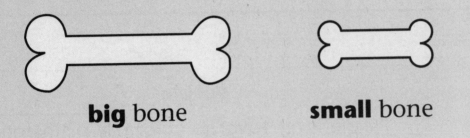

big bone   **small** bone

A Circle each adjective that describes size.

1. short neck

2. big legs

3. small brain

4. long tail

5. large head

6. tiny arms

© Pearson Education

B Write the adjectives that describe size.

_____

1. long green stem   _____

_____

2. tiny red petals   _____

_____

3. short round leaves _____

C Write three sentences about the giraffe.
Use adjectives to tell about its size.

_____

_____

_____

_____

_____

_____

© Pearson Education

Test Preparation

✓ **Mark** the sentence that has a line under the adjective.

1. ○ The <u>rabbit</u> has a short tail.
   ○ The rabbit has a <u>short</u> tail.
   ○ The rabbit <u>has</u> a short tail.

2. ○ <u>It</u> has very long ears!
   ○ It <u>has</u> very long ears!
   ○ It has very <u>long</u> ears!

3. ○ A <u>guppy</u> is a little fish.
   ○ A guppy is a <u>little</u> fish.
   ○ A guppy is a little <u>fish</u>.

4. ○ It <u>swims</u> in a huge bowl.
   ○ It swims in a huge <u>bowl</u>.
   ○ It swims in a <u>huge</u> bowl.

5. ○ The fish has <u>tiny</u> eyes.
   ○ The fish <u>has</u> tiny eyes.
   ○ The fish has tiny <u>eyes</u>.

© Pearson Education

Review

 Circle each adjective that describes size.

    1. small cat

    2. tall tree

    3. long snake

    4. short flower

Look at the pictures. **Write** the adjective in ( ) that tells about each picture.

5. _____ animal

       (long, short)

6. _____ animal

       (huge, tiny)

7. _____ bird

       (big, small)

8. _____ bird

       (short, tall)

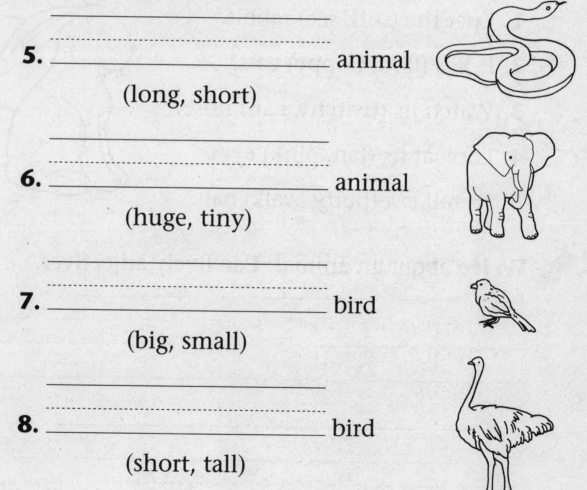

© Pearson Education

Lively Adjectives

Lively adjectives describe things in an interesting way. They make your writing more fun to read.

She brushed the dog's <u>silky</u> fur.

It licked her with its <u>wet</u> tongue.

 Circle the adjective in ( ) to complete each sentence.

1. I pet the (soft, see) rabbit.

2. It has (bird, floppy) ears.

3. Watch its (twitchy, can) nose.

4. Look at its (fan, pink) eyes.

5. Its tail is a (puffy, walk) ball.

Write about an animal. **Use** lively adjectives.

_____

_____

_____

_____

© Pearson Education

Describe a Scary Animal

Writing Prompt   Describe a scary animal. Use lively adjectives to describe this animal.

First sentence tells what the animal is.

Lively adjectives tell why this animal was scary.

All sentences focus on this animal.

T. Rex

T. rex was a creature with a huge head. It had sharp teeth and strong jaws. There were claws on its feet. Its heavy tail could smash smaller animals.

© Pearson Education

Adjectives for What Kind

An **adjective** can tell what kind.

bright moon

happy children

A **Circle** the adjective that tells what kind.

1. We get together in cold weather.

2. Uncle Lu cooks hot chili.

3. Grandma gets out warm quilts.

4. Aunt Bet tells funny stories.

5. Mom sings old songs.

6. I show them new dances.

7. Mom and I make spicy dip.

8. We eat it with crisp crackers.

© Pearson Education

B **Write** the adjective that tells what kind.

1. Put on fuzzy hats. _____

2. Find thick mittens. _____

3. Pull on heavy boots. _____

C **Write** three sentences about what you do in summer. **Use** adjectives such as *hot*, *warm*, and *wet*.

_____

_____

_____

_____

_____

_____

© Pearson Education

Test Preparation

☑ **Mark** the sentence that has a line under the adjective.

1. ○ Jenna <u>likes</u> a clean room.
   ○ Jenna likes a <u>clean</u> room.
   ○ Jenna likes a clean <u>room</u>.

2. ○ She helps me with my messy <u>room</u>.
   ○ She <u>helps</u> me with my messy room.
   ○ She helps me with my <u>messy</u> room.

3. ○ I <u>love</u> fresh snow in winter.
   ○ I love <u>fresh</u> snow in winter.
   ○ I love fresh snow in <u>winter</u>.

4. ○ I help Jenna with her <u>new</u> sled.
   ○ I help <u>Jenna</u> with her new sled.
   ○ I <u>help</u> Jenna with her new sled.

5. ○ We <u>race</u> down the icy hill.
   ○ We race down the icy <u>hill</u>.
   ○ We race down the <u>icy</u> hill.

© Pearson Education

Review

 Circle the adjective that tells what kind.

1. Mike knows silly jokes.

2. Dirty dogs need baths.

3. Fall has cool days.

4. She wore shiny beads.

5. Kittens have soft fur.

Choose the adjective in ( ) that completes each sentence correctly. **Write** the adjective on the line.

6. My bed has _____ sheets.

(smooth, happy)

7. The _____ camera does not work.

(old, bright)

8. _____ music hurt my ears.

(Wet, Loud)

© Pearson Education

Persuasive Words

When you **persuade,** you try to get someone to do something. **Persuasive words** such as *should, must, need, best,* and *important* can help you.

Circle the words that persuade in the letter.

March 25, 2007

Dear Aunt Celia,
  You should come to my birthday. It is an important day for me. I'm having the best party ever. Please come.

                    Love,
                    Leo

Write a note to a friend about something you want him or her to do. **Use** words that persuade.

_____

_____

_____

_____

_____

_____

© Pearson Education

Write an Ad

Writing Prompt Write an ad for a new healthful snack. Give this snack a name. Use words to make readers want to buy it.

This snack has an interesting name.

Ad tells what snack looks like.

Words are used to persuade people to buy the snack.

Choco-Beans

Choco-Beans will make you healthy.

These green chips taste like candy.

Each bag has the vitamins of 1 pound of green beans.

You must try this snack.

© Pearson Education

Adjectives for How Many

Some **adjectives** tell how many.

one boy

two chairs

A **Draw** lines from the words to the pictures.

1. one mother

2. five babies

3. three sisters

4. two fathers

5. four brothers

© Pearson Education

B **Write** the adjective that tells how many.

1. Angie has one sister. _____

2. Six children came. _____

3. We saw ten dads. _____

C **Look** at the picture. **Complete** each sentence with an adjective from the box.

two	three	four

4. There are _____ dogs.

5. There are _____ cats.

6. There are _____ black dogs.

© Pearson Education

Test Preparation

✓ **Mark** the sentence that has a line under the adjective.

1. ○ <u>Six</u> friends came to dinner.
   ○ Six <u>friends</u> came to dinner.
   ○ Six friends <u>came</u> to dinner.

2. ○ Three children <u>drank</u> milk.
   ○ <u>Three</u> children drank milk.
   ○ Three <u>children</u> drank milk.

3. ○ <u>Two</u> sisters sat together.
   ○ Two sisters <u>sat</u> together.
   ○ Two <u>sisters</u> sat together.

4. ○ The <u>men</u> washed ten dishes.
   ○ The men washed <u>ten</u> dishes.
   ○ The men <u>washed</u> ten dishes.

5. ○ All nine friends <u>had</u> a good time!
   ○ All <u>nine</u> friends had a good time!
   ○ All nine friends had a good <u>time</u>!

© Pearson Education

Review

✓ **Circle** the adjective that tells how many.

1. We picked ten apples.

2. Mom read six books.

3. I played with five toy cars.

4. Dad packed eight boxes.

✓ **Choose** the correct adjective from the box. **Write** the adjective on the line.

one	two	three	four

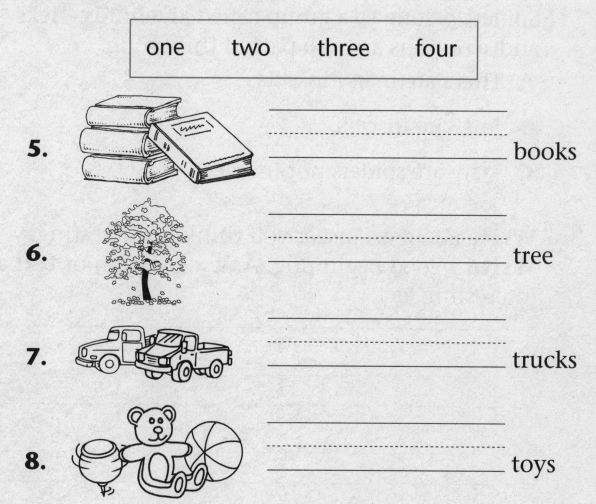

5. _____ books

6. _____ tree

7. _____ trucks

8. _____ toys

© Pearson Education

Good Beginnings

A **good beginning** makes readers want to read more. Here are two ways you can begin your writing.

- Ask a question.
- Tell an interesting fact.

Underline the best beginning for the paragraph.

Insects have six legs. Spiders have eight legs. Spiders belong to a group called arachnids. Ticks and scorpions are also part of this group.

A There are many insects.

B Ants are insects.

C Why are spiders not insects?

Write about an insect you think is interesting. **Write** a good beginning. **Ask** a question or **tell** an interesting fact.

_____

_____

_____

_____

_____

_____

© Pearson Education

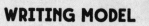
Write a Sign

> **Writing Prompt** Think of something you want to protect. Make a sign to warn people to be careful.

First sentence gets reader's attention.

Sign is focused on the baby brother.

Sentences are clear and smooth.

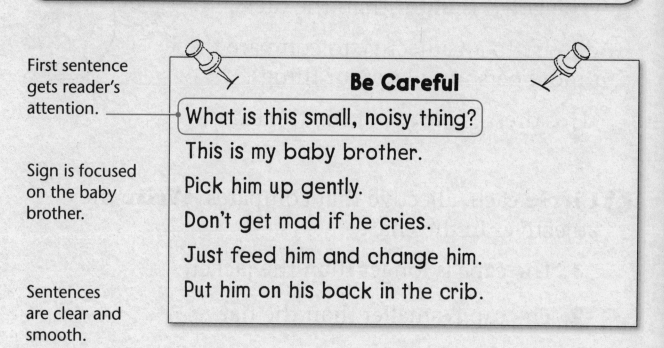

Be Careful

What is this small, noisy thing?

This is my baby brother.

Pick him up gently.

Don't get mad if he cries.

Just feed him and change him.

Put him on his back in the crib.

© Pearson Education

Adjectives That Compare

Add **-er** to an adjective to compare two persons, places, or things.

The gown is **older** than the dress.

Add **-est** to an adjective to compare three or more persons, places, or things.

This dress is **oldest** of the three.

A **Circle** each adjective that compares. **Write** the adjectives in the chart.

1. The cape is longer than the jacket.

2. The cap is smaller than the hat.

3. Which is the longest wig of the three?

4. I found the smallest coat of all.

Adjectives with *-er*	Adjectives with *-est*

© Pearson Education

B **Add** -er or -est to the word in ( ). **Write** the new word on the line.

1. I am (slow) than John.

_____

2. Pam is (fast) of all.

_____

3. Pam is (short) than John. _____

C **Write** about three things in your room that are special to you. **Use** words from the box or your own adjectives that compare.

| oldest | longer | newer | shortest | smaller |

_____

_____

_____

_____

_____

_____

© Pearson Education

Test Preparation

☑ **Mark** the sentence that has a line under the adjective.

1. ○ Sarah is oldest of all my <u>friends</u>.
   ○ <u>Sarah</u> is oldest of all my friends.
   ○ Sarah is <u>oldest</u> of all my friends.

2. ○ She has a <u>smaller</u> house than I do.
   ○ She has a smaller <u>house</u> than I do.
   ○ She <u>has</u> a smaller house than I do.

3. ○ We have the greenest <u>grass</u> on our street.
   ○ We have the <u>greenest</u> grass on our street.
   ○ We have the greenest grass on our <u>street</u>.

4. ○ <u>Kip</u> is the loudest dog in the neighborhood.
   ○ Kip is the loudest <u>dog</u> in the neighborhood.
   ○ Kip is the <u>loudest</u> dog in the neighborhood.

5. ○ Is your street <u>longer</u> than mine?
   ○ <u>Is</u> your street longer than mine?
   ○ Is your <u>street</u> longer than mine?

© Pearson Education

Review

✓ **Circle** each adjective that compares. **Write** the adjectives in the chart.

1. My hair is longer than her hair.

2. Ann's hair is longest of all.

3. He is shorter than I am.

4. Sam is shortest of all.

Adjectives with *-er*	Adjectives with *-est*
_____	_____
_____	_____
_____	_____

✓ **Add** *-er* or *-est* to the word in ( ).
Write the new word on the line.

5. I am _____ than my sister. (old)

6. Grandma is _____ of all. (old)

© Pearson Education

Word Choice

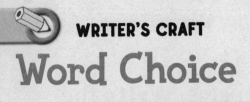

Choose words to make your writing clear and interesting.

No   Mom gave me a nice shirt.

Yes   Mom gave me a pale blue shirt.

 Underline the sentence that sounds more interesting.

1. My closet is full of clothes and toys.

My closet is full of stuff.

2. I can't find the pretty skirt.

I can't find the ruffled skirt.

3. Where is my purple vest?

Where is my purple thing?

Describe your room. **Choose** your words carefully.

_____

_____

_____

_____

_____

_____

© Pearson Education

Describe Something Special

Writing Prompt Describe something that is special to you. Tell why it is special.

Writer explains why the ring is special.

Words give exact details.

Adjective that compares shows what the writer thinks of the ring.

A Special Ring

I have a very special ring. Mom bought it for me at an art fair. It is special to me because it has a pearl. That is my birthstone. My ring is beautiful. This is the greatest present I ever got.

© Pearson Education

Commands

A **command** is a sentence that tells someone to do something. It begins with a **capital letter**. It ends with a **period (.)**.

Run fast.

Please stop the dog.

A **Underline** each sentence that is a command.

1. I broke a plate.

2. Pick up all the pieces.

3. Can you help me?

4. Please find the glue.

5. Put the pieces on the table.

6. One piece is missing.

7. Watch me fix the plate.

8. How does it look?

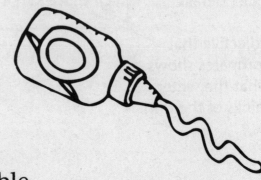

© Pearson Education

B **Rewrite** each sentence as a command.

Example   You can help me.
                 Help me.

1. You can look under the bed.

_____

- - - - - - - - - - - - - - - - -

_____

2. You can go into the closet.

_____

- - - - - - - - - - - - - - - - -

_____

3. You can find the cat.

_____

- - - - - - - - - - - - - - - - -

_____

C Ming has a problem. What should Ming do? **Write** commands.

4. Fix

_____

- - - - - - - - - - - - - - - - -

_____

5. Use

_____

- - - - - - - - - - - - - - - - -

_____

6. Ask

_____

- - - - - - - - - - - - - - - - -

_____

© Pearson Education

Test Preparation

 Mark the sentence that is a command.

1. ○ My glove has a hole in it.
   ○ Fix the hole in my glove.
   ○ Did you find the hole?

2. ○ Please check the mailbox.
   ○ Did the mail come today?
   ○ I will check the mailbox.

3. ○ Is that letter for me?
   ○ Read me the name on the letter.
   ○ I will read the name on the letter.

4. ○ I lost the dog.
   ○ Is the dog lost?
   ○ Tell me who lost the dog.

5. ○ Please look for the dog outside.
   ○ Do you see the dog outside?
   ○ The dog is outside.

© Pearson Education

Review

 Circle the command. **Draw** a picture for the command.

1. Where is my shoe?

2. Give me my shoe.

3. I want my shoe.

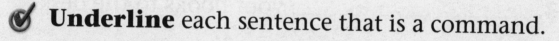 **Underline** each sentence that is a command.

4. Is it dark in here?

5. Turn on the lights.

6. What was that?

7. Please open the window.

8. Look over there.

9. I saw something.

10. Give me the phone.

© Pearson Education

Use Commands in Writing

Use all kinds of sentences when you write. **Use commands** as well as statements and questions.

Write commands. **Use** verbs from the box.

Take	Sit	Give

1. _____ me that book, please.

2. _____ at this table with us.

3. _____ your books to the desk.

Write about something you need to do. **Use** a command to get a friend to help you.

_____

_____

_____

_____

_____

© Pearson Education

Write a Letter of Advice

Writing Prompt   Read the letter from "Tired." Write a letter giving advice to "Tired."

> Dear Annie Advice,
>
>   My neighbor's dog barks all night long. I cannot get any sleep. What should I do?
>
>   Tired

Writing follows the correct letter form.

Writer focuses on the problem.

Sentences are clear commands.

How to Get Some Sleep
Dear Tired,
Talk to the dog's owner. Talk to your other neighbors. Close the windows. Play music. Get earplugs.
Annie Advice

© Pearson Education

Exclamations

An **exclamation** is a sentence that shows strong feeling. It begins with a **capital letter.** It ends with an **exclamation mark (!)**.

That baby bird is in trouble!

A **Write** each exclamation correctly.

1. the bird fell out of its nest

_____

- -

_____

2. the bird is hurt

_____

- -

_____

3. we should help it

_____

- -

_____

4. it is flying again

_____

- -

_____

© Pearson Education

B **Read** each pair of sentences. **Write** each exclamation on the line.

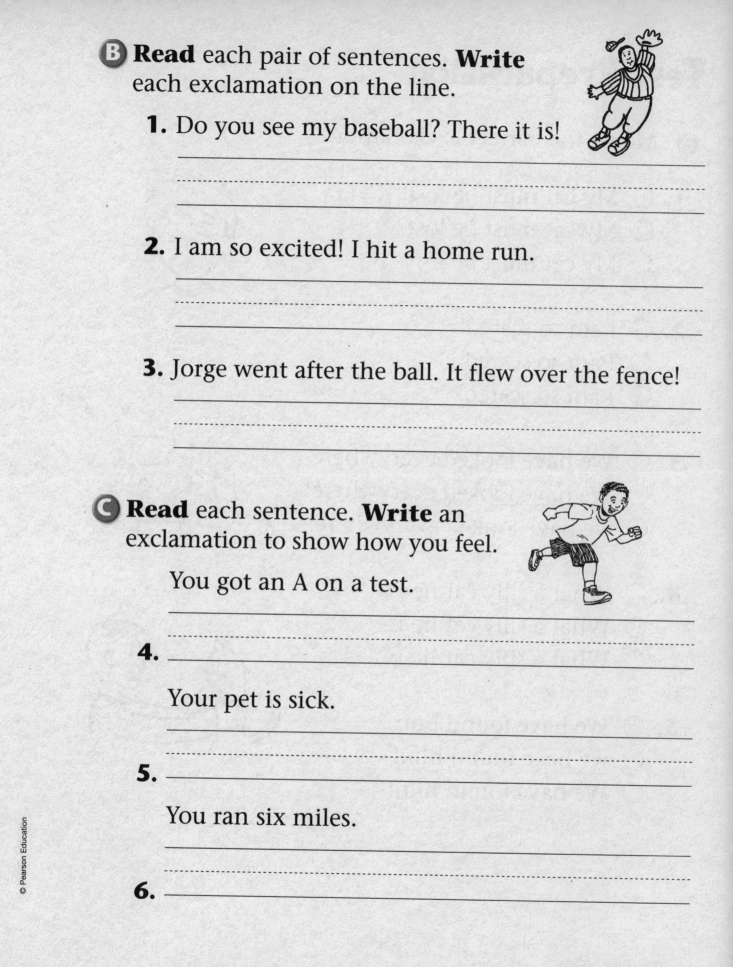

1. Do you see my baseball? There it is!

_____

- -

_____

2. I am so excited! I hit a home run.

_____

- -

_____

3. Jorge went after the ball. It flew over the fence!

_____

- -

_____

C **Read** each sentence. **Write** an exclamation to show how you feel.

You got an A on a test.

_____

4. -

_____

Your pet is sick.

_____

5. -

_____

You ran six miles.

_____

6. -

_____

© Pearson Education

Test Preparation

✓ **Mark** the correct exclamation.

1. ○ My cat must be lost!
   ○ My cat must be lost?
   ○ My cat must be lost

2. ○ i am so scared!
   ○ I am so scared
   ○ I am so scared!

3. ○ We have looked everywhere
   ○ We have looked everywhere!
   ○ we have looked everywhere!

4. ○ What a silly cat he is
   ○ What a silly cat he is!
   ○ What a silly cat he is?

5. ○ We have found him
   ○ we have found him!
   ○ We have found him!

© Pearson Education

Review

✔ **Read** each pair of sentences.
Write the exclamation on the line.

1. I look for Tina. What a good friend she is!

_____

- -

_____

2. We play games. She is so much fun!

_____

- -

_____

3. Tina is not here! Where is she?

_____

- -

_____

✔ **Write** each exclamation correctly.

4. i am so sad

_____

- -

_____

5. here comes Tina

_____

- -

_____

© Pearson Education

Use Exclamations in Writing

Let readers know how you feel about something.
Use exclamations to show feelings.

Circle the sentences that are exclamations.

1. My sleepover is on Friday night.

2. Can you come?

3. It will be great!

4. Be at my house by 6.

5. I can't wait!

Tell a friend about something that happened this week. **Use** an exclamation to show how you feel.

_____

_____

_____

_____

_____

_____

_____

_____

© Pearson Education

Write a Report

Writing Prompt Write a report about an animal. Include interesting facts about this animal.

This report has interesting facts about moles.

An exclamation makes a good beginning.

Word choice makes the writing lively.

Amazing Moles

Moles are amazing animals! They live underground and dig tunnels. Their front legs work like shovels. They are very fast diggers. Moles are almost blind, but they hear very well.

© Pearson Education

How Sentences Begin and End

A **sentence** is a group of words that tells a complete idea. It begins with a **capital letter**. A statement ends with a **period (.)**. A **question** ends with a **question mark (?)**.

This is an acorn**.**

How did it get here**?**

A **Circle** each group of words that is a complete sentence.

1. Where is it?

2. We will look here.

3. Find a clue?

4. By the sink.

5. I see something.

6. A little note.

7. What does it say?

8. It has numbers.

© Pearson Education

B **Write** the sentences on the lines.
Begin and **end** each sentence correctly.

1. did the acorn fly

_____

- - - - - - - - - - - - - - - - - - - -

_____

2. it is a mystery

_____

- - - - - - - - - - - - - - - - - - - -

_____

3. does it have wings

_____

- - - - - - - - - - - - - - - - - - - -

_____

C **Change** each statement to a question. **Write** the new sentence on the line. An example is shown below.

Example   She is looking for it.
Is she looking for it?

4. It can hide.

_____

- - - - - - - - - - - - - - - - - - - -

_____

5. We will find it.

_____

- - - - - - - - - - - - - - - - - - - -

_____

© Pearson Education

Test Preparation

 Mark the group of words that is a complete sentence and is written correctly.

1. ○ What is in?
   ○ What is in the tree?
   ○ what is in the tree?

2. ○ Ben will look.
   ○ Will look.
   ○ Ben will look

3. ○ A bird?
   ○ is it a bird?
   ○ Is it a bird?

4. ○ Maybe it is a cat.
   ○ Maybe a cat.
   ○ maybe it is a cat.

5. ○ I can see the.
   ○ I can see the long tail
   ○ I can see the long tail.

© Pearson Education

Review

© Pearson Education

 Circle each group of words that is a complete sentence.

1. Looking for a clue.

2. Is that a clue?

3. It is a footprint.

4. Will look at.

5. Who did it?

 Change each statement to a question. **Write** the new sentence on the line. An example is shown below.

    Example   She is waiting there.
                    Is she waiting there?

6. Katie is a detective.

_____

_____

7. She will find the ring.

_____

_____

8. It was under the table.

_____

_____

Make Writing Less Wordy

- Don't use phrases such as *kind of, I think that,* and *it seems like.*

- Don't use *a lot of.* Use *many* or another word.

- Don't use two words that mean the same thing: ~~great~~ big, ~~little~~ tiny.

- Don't use several words when you can use one word: moved ~~with great quickness~~, moved quickly.

Underline the sentences that are less wordy.

1. I think that Kurt has a lot of toys.

Kurt has many toys.

2. That big dog is scary.

That great big dog is kind of scary.

Write about a trip you have made. **Use** only as many words as are needed.

_____

_____

_____

_____

© Pearson Education

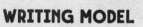

Write a Job Description

Writing Prompt Write a job description. Name the job, and write sentences showing what kind of person would be good at this job.

Title tells what the job is.

Adjectives tell what kind of person would be good at this job.

There are no unnecessary words.

Detective Wanted

Are you curious and careful?

Do you look at things closely?

Do you understand people?

Do you know how to blend in?

If you said Yes to these questions, you might make a good detective.

© Pearson Education

Pronouns

A **pronoun** is a word that takes the place of a noun or nouns. The words *he, she, it, we, you,* and *they* are pronouns.

The box is heavy. ⟶ **It** is heavy.

Dan and I need help. ⟶ **We** need help.

Ⓐ Circle the pronoun in each sentence.

1. Henry and he push the box.

2. Will you help?

3. We will make a ramp.

4. Is it ready yet?

5. Ann says she is ready.

6. He packs more boxes.

7. They are by the door.

8. Can we wait until later?

9. Then she can help too.

10. Soon it will be done.

© Pearson Education

B **Circle** the pronoun in ( ) that can take the place of the underlined word or words.

1. Ellen pushes a box. <u>Ellen</u> uses a ramp. (She, We)

2. Jim pulls a box up. <u>Jim</u> uses a pulley. (They, He)

3. A wedge is a simple machine. <u>A wedge</u> is slanted. (It, You)

4. Mai and I lift the box. <u>Mai and I</u> use a lever. (He, We)

5. Wheels are round. <u>Wheels</u> help things move. (They, She)

C **Change** the underlined word or words. **Use** *she, they,* or *it.* **Write** the new sentences.

6. <u>A wagon</u> has wheels.

_____

_____

7. <u>Mai</u> pulls the wagon.

_____

_____

8. <u>Jim and Jake</u> push the wagon.

_____

_____

© Pearson Education

Test Preparation

 Mark the pronoun that can replace the underlined word or words.

1. <u>Kay</u> rides a bike.
   - ○ It
   - ○ She
   - ○ They

2. <u>The bike</u> is new.
   - ○ We
   - ○ He
   - ○ It

3. <u>Kay and I</u> ride together.
   - ○ We
   - ○ He
   - ○ She

4. <u>Alex and Jane</u> ride too.
   - ○ We
   - ○ You
   - ○ They

5. Tomorrow <u>Kevin</u> will ride.
   - ○ it
   - ○ he
   - ○ they

© Pearson Education

Review

 Circle the pronoun in each sentence.

1. We can move the box.

2. Will you find the ramp?

3. It is not too heavy.

4. He will put the ramp here.

5. Can they work together?

Change the underlined word or words to a pronoun from the box. **Write** the new sentence on the line.

She	We	He

6. <u>Rob</u> digs in the dirt.

_____

- -

_____

7. <u>Pam</u> makes holes.

_____

- -

_____

8. <u>Sue and I</u> put in the plants.

_____

- -

_____

© Pearson Education

Supporting Details

The main idea of a paragraph is what the paragraph is about. **Supporting details** tell more about the main idea. Every sentence should tell a supporting detail.

Read the paragraph. **Write** the letter of the supporting detail that belongs in the paragraph.

Did your garden give you too many vegetables? Here's what you can do. Give them to friends. Take the vegetables to a local food bank. _____

A Plant more seeds to grow more vegetables.

B Make them into soup and freeze it.

C Buy vegetables at the grocery store.

Write two detail sentences that support one of these main ideas.

Fish make great pets.   Fish make bad pets.

_____

_____

_____

_____

_____

_____

© Pearson Education

Write an Explanation

Writing Prompt Think of a machine in your home. What does it do? How does it make your life easier?

Explanation begins with a main idea sentence.

Detail sentences support the main idea.

Last sentence ties the other sentences together.

Vacuum Cleaner

A vacuum cleaner cleans our apartment.

It pulls dirt out of rugs. It sucks up things we drop on the floor. It even gets Pepper's hairs off the chair. We would have a lot more mess without a vacuum cleaner.

© Pearson Education

Using *I* and *Me*

The pronouns **I** and **me** take the place of your name. Use **I** in the naming part of a sentence. Use **me** in the action part. Always write **I** with a capital letter.

I invent things. My friend Kim helps **me**.

When you talk about yourself and another person, name yourself last. The pronouns **I** and **me** take the place of your name.

Kim and **I** try my new toy. Josh helps Kim and **me**.

A **Circle** the correct word or words in ( ) to complete each sentence.

1. (I, Me) make old things into new things.

2. Josh gave (I, me) his old bike.

3. (I, Me) had a great idea.

4. Kim and (I, me) made a rocket ship.

5. Watch Kim and (I, me) blast off!

6. (Kim and I, I and Kim) will go to the moon.

© Pearson Education

B **Write** *I* or *me* to complete each sentence.

1. _____ will make a kite.

2. You can help _____.

3. You and _____ will fly the kite.

C **Write** about something you have made. It might be a game, food, or toy. **Use** *I* and *me*.

_____

_____

_____

_____

_____

_____

_____

© Pearson Education

Test Preparation

✓ **Mark** the word or words that complete each sentence.

1. ___ built a block house.
- ○ Ned and me
- ○ Ned and I
- ○ Me

2. ___ liked the windows.
- ○ Me
- ○ Mom and me
- ○ I

3. Mom got ___ some more blocks.
- ○ Nan and me
- ○ me and Nan
- ○ I

4. ___ made more rooms.
- ○ Mom and me
- ○ Me
- ○ Mom and I

5. ___ put flowers in the yard.
- ○ I
- ○ Nan and me
- ○ Me

© Pearson Education

Review

© Pearson Education

 Circle the correct pronoun in ( ) that completes each sentence. **Circle** the picture that answers the riddle.

1. (I, me) am big.

2. You can pat (I, me).

3. Hear (I, me) bark.

4. What am (I, me)?

 **Write** *I* or *me* to complete each sentence.

5. Sue made _____ a picture.

6. _____ put it in my bag.

7. Sue and _____ raced with Tom.

8. She always beats Tom and _____.

Include All Information

> **Include all information** that readers need to know.
> In an invitation, include the date, time, and place.

Read the invitation below. Add the missing information.

Cody Davis Is Having a Party!	
For	his 7th birthday
	_____
Date	_____
	_____
	_____
Time	_____
Place	3431 Doyle Road

Write a note inviting a friend to do something.
Include all the information.

_____

_____

_____

_____

_____

_____

© Pearson Education

Give an Award

Writing Prompt Give an award to a famous person. The person can be living or dead. Tell why this person deserves the award.

Writer gives information about what Bell did.

Pronouns are used correctly.

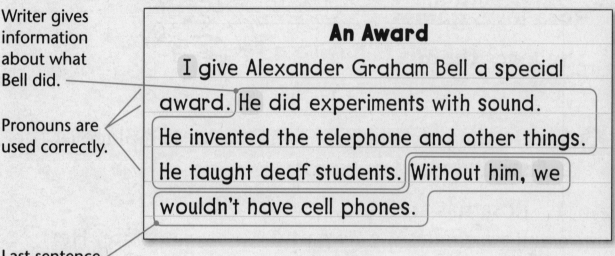

An Award

I give Alexander Graham Bell a special award. He did experiments with sound. He invented the telephone and other things. He taught deaf students. Without him, we wouldn't have cell phones.

Last sentence connects Bell to phones used today.

© Pearson Education

More About Pronouns

A **pronoun** can take the place of some words in a sentence. *I, you, he, she, it, we,* and *they* are used in the *naming part* of a sentence. *Me, you, him, her, it, us,* and *them* are used in the *action part* of a sentence.

Rosa loves **games**.

She loves **them**.

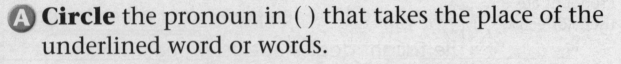

A **Circle** the pronoun in ( ) that takes the place of the underlined word or words.

1. Rosa has an idea.
   <u>Rosa</u> makes a new game.   (She, Her)

2. I will help Rosa.
   Sean will help <u>Rosa</u> too.   (she, her)

3. Sean and I play the game.
   <u>Sean and I</u> like it.   (We, Us)

4. The game is fast.
   <u>The game</u> is fun.   (You, It)

5. Rosa thanks Sean and me.
   Rosa gives <u>Sean and me</u> the game. (we, us)

© Pearson Education

B Write the pronoun in ( ) that can take the place of the underlined word or words.

_____

1. <u>Pam</u> makes a toy. (She, Her) _____

_____

2. <u>The toy</u> does not work. (He, It) _____

_____

3. I fix the toy for <u>Pam</u>. (she, her) _____

C Imagine you make something with a friend. **Write** about what happens. **Use** the pronouns _it, he, him, she, her, I, me, we,_ or _us._

_____

_____

_____

_____

_____

_____

_____

© Pearson Education

Test Preparation

 Mark the pronoun that can replace the underlined word or words.

1. <u>Tom</u> has an idea for a game.

- ○ Her
- ○ We
- ○ He

2. <u>Tom and I</u> work together.

- ○ We
- ○ Us
- ○ Them

3. My parents see <u>Tom and me</u>.

- ○ he
- ○ us
- ○ we

4. <u>My parents</u> help with the game.

- ○ They
- ○ We
- ○ Them

5. We let <u>my parents</u> play the game.

- ○ we
- ○ us
- ○ them

© Pearson Education

Review

 Write the pronoun from the box that can replace the underlined word or words in each sentence.

We	him	He

_____

1. <u>Will</u> made a kite. _____

2. I helped <u>Will</u>. _____

3. <u>Will and I</u> flew the kite. _____

✓ **Change** the underlined word or words to a pronoun in ( ). **Write** the new sentence.

4. <u>Kim</u> has a kite. (She, Her)

_____

_____

5. <u>Kim and Al</u> need wind. (Them, They)

_____

_____

© Pearson Education

Sentences

> • Use all kinds of **sentences**: statements, questions, commands, and exclamations.
> • Start sentences with different words.

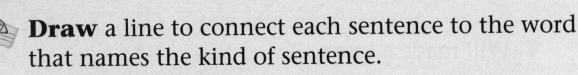 **Draw** a line to connect each sentence to the word that names the kind of sentence.

1. What invention do I want?   Statement

2. I want a time machine.   Question

3. It would be so exciting!   Command

4. Visit the past with me.   Exclamation

Begin the sentence with the underlined word. **Write** the paragraph.

Example   He had an idea <u>yesterday</u>.
Answer   Yesterday he had an idea.

He made a model <u>today</u>. He changed it <u>later</u>. He is happy with it <u>now</u>.

_____

_____

_____

_____

© Pearson Education

Tell About an Invention

> **Writing Prompt**   Think of an invention you would like to make. Write what this invention could do. Give it a name.

This invention has a good name.

This tells what the invention can do.

Different kinds of sentences make the writing lively.

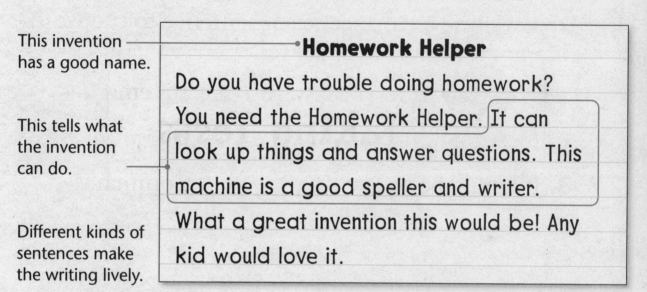

Homework Helper

Do you have trouble doing homework? You need the Homework Helper. It can look up things and answer questions. This machine is a good speller and writer. What a great invention this would be! Any kid would love it.

Can I help you with your homework?

© Pearson Education

Taking Tests

Follow these tips when writing for a test.

Before Writing

- Read the prompt carefully. Think about what it asks you to do.

- Write down key words. For example, here is a prompt:

  Write a <u>thank-you letter</u> to a <u>friend</u>.

  The key words tell you to write a letter to thank a friend. You will use the letter form and thank someone in a friendly voice.

- Use a graphic organizer to plan your composition.

During Writing

- Keep the prompt in mind to stay on the topic.

- Follow your graphic organizer. Stay focused.

- Write a good beginning. You might ask readers a question or give an interesting fact.

- Support your main idea.

- Write a strong ending. You might add a final comment of your own or give your reader a command.

After Writing

- Check grammar, punctuation, and spelling.

- Are there places that need more details or clearer information?

Writing a Story About Me

A **test** may ask you to write a story about yourself. Your story should have a beginning, middle, and end. Follow the tips below.

Know what you need to do.

Read the directions carefully.

Write a story about one of your favorite things.

Find a good topic.

Pick a favorite thing that you can write more than one sentence about. Think of your favorite game, animal, food, or color.

Put your ideas in order.

Think of a beginning, middle, and end.

You can use a story chart like the one below.

Favorite Food—Pizza

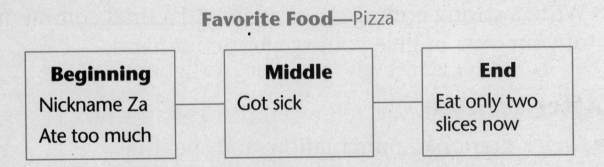

Beginning	**Middle**	**End**
Nickname Za	Got sick	Eat only two
Ate too much		slices now

Write a good beginning.

Make readers want to keep reading.

Develop your ideas.

Work from your story chart.

Write a clear ending.

Let readers know you have finished.

Check your work.

You can add or change words neatly.

The story below is about a favorite thing.
It uses the story chart.

1 — **How did I get the nickname Za?** That is
what I called pizza when I was little. One time
2 — I ate four slices. Then I got sick. I felt like I
3 — would pop. Now I only eat two slices. Pizza is
still my favorite food — but not too much! — 4

1. Writer starts with an interesting question.

2. *Then* and *Now* tell when things happened.

3. *Pop* shows how the writer felt.

4. This is a clear ending.

Writing a How-To Report

A **test** may ask you to write a how-to report. Be sure to include all the steps. Use words such as *first* and *next* to show the order of the steps. Follow the tips below.

Know what you need to do.

Read the directions carefully.

Tell how to make or do something. Keep the steps simple. Put them in order.

Find a good topic.

Think of something you made. Remember each step.

Put your ideas in order.

List your steps in a how-to chart. Use words such as *first, next,* and *last* to show order.

How to Make a Ball-Toss Game

What you need: Large box, tennis ball

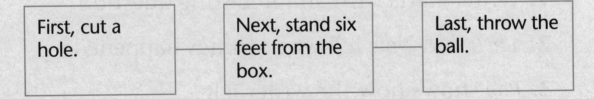

First, cut a hole. — Next, stand six feet from the box. — Last, throw the ball.

Write a good beginning.

Tell readers what is being made.

Develop your ideas.

Work from your chart. Add details. Make sure your directions are complete.

Write a clear ending.

Let readers know when you have finished by using a word such as *last* or *finally*.

Check your work.

You can add or change words neatly.

The report below is about a game.
It uses the how-to chart.

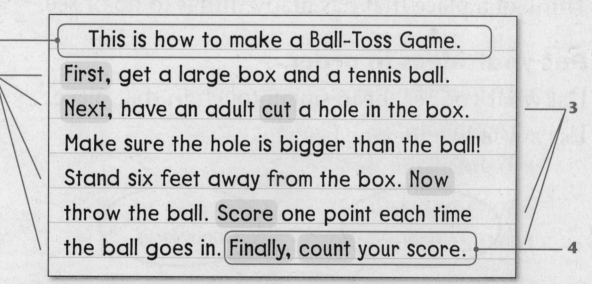

1 — This is how to make a Ball-Toss Game.

2 — First, get a large box and a tennis ball.

Next, have an adult cut a hole in the box.

Make sure the hole is bigger than the ball!

Stand six feet away from the box. Now

throw the ball. Score one point each time

the ball goes in. Finally, count your score.

3

4

1. Writer starts by telling what the game is.

2. *First, Next, Now,* and *Finally* show the order of steps.

3. Verbs tell what to do.

4. Ending tells the last step.

Writing a Description

> A **test** may ask you to tell about a place. Use words to give a picture of this place. Follow the tips below.

Know what you need to do.

Read the directions carefully.

> Tell about a place you like. Describe what you see, hear, smell, or touch there.

Find a good topic.

Pick a favorite place that you can write about.

Think of a place that has many things to do or see.

Put your ideas in order.

List what you see, hear, smell, touch in that place.

Use a web like the one below.

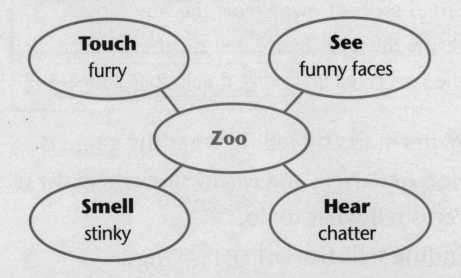

Write a good beginning.

You might start by asking a question.

Develop your ideas.

Add details from your web.

Write a clear ending.

Wrap up your ideas in your last sentence.

Check your work.

You can add or take out words.
The description below is a about a place.
It uses ideas from the web.

1 — Do you like the zoo as much as I do?

2 — My favorite animals at Lincoln Zoo are the monkeys. They chatter. This must be how they — 3
talk. They make funny faces. There was a
furry monkey in the petting zoo. Some animals — 4
smell stinky, but I love the zoo anyway.

1. Writer starts with a good question.

2. Nouns give readers clear pictures.

3. These words tell what the writer sees, hears, smells, and touches.

4. Ending tells the writer's feelings.

Writing a Persuasive Letter

A **test** may ask you to write a letter to persuade someone to do something.

Follow the tips below.

Know what you need to do.

Read the directions carefully.

> Write a letter to persuade a friend to play a pretending game. Your letter should have all the letter parts.

Find a good topic. What do you like to pretend?

Put your ideas in order. Include all the letter parts.

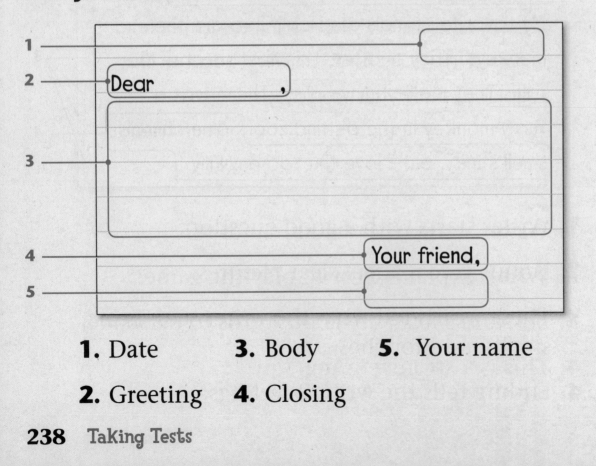

1   Dear   ,

2

3

4   Your friend,

5

1. Date   **3.** Body   **5.** Your name

2. Greeting   **4.** Closing

Write a good beginning. Try a command.

Develop your ideas.

Give reasons why your friend should play.

Write a clear ending. End with a bang.

Check your work. Make changes neatly.

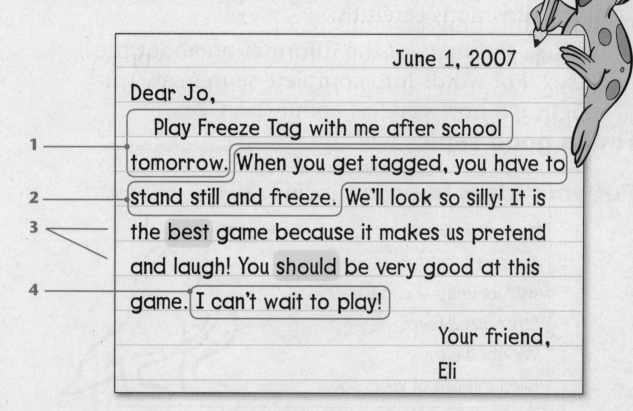

June 1, 2007

Dear Jo,

1 — Play Freeze Tag with me after school tomorrow. When you get tagged, you have to

2 — stand still and freeze. We'll look so silly! It is

3 — the best game because it makes us pretend and laugh! You should be very good at this

4 — game. I can't wait to play!

Your friend,

Eli

1. Writer starts with a command.

2. Writer explains how to play the game.

3. *Best* and *should* are good words to persuade.

4. This is a strong ending.

Writing a Summary

A **test** may ask you to sum up information from a chart. Use complete sentences. Include all the important information. Follow the tips below.

Know what you need to do.

Read the directions carefully.

> Write a summary of the information about the T. rex. Put words into complete sentences. You might tell how you feel about the T. rex.

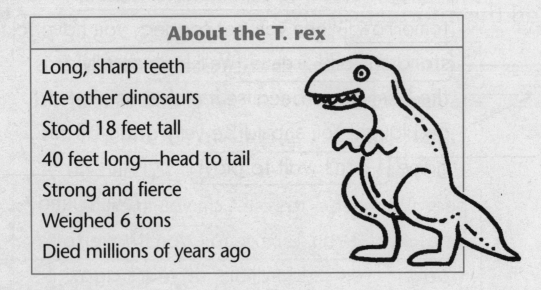

About the T. rex

Long, sharp teeth

Ate other dinosaurs

Stood 18 feet tall

40 feet long—head to tail

Strong and fierce

Weighed 6 tons

Died millions of years ago

Put your ideas in order.

Decide in what order to put the facts in your summary.

Write a good beginning.

You might begin with an interesting fact or question.

Develop your ideas.

Write complete sentences about the facts in the chart.

Write a clear ending.

Write a strong ending. Let readers know you are done.

Check your work.

You can add or change words neatly.

The report below is about the T. rex. It uses the picture and the information given.

1 — Which dinosaur is your favorite? Mine is
2 — T. rex because it was strong and fierce.
It had long, sharp teeth to eat other
dinosaurs. T. rex was 18 feet tall and 40
feet from head to tail! Can you imagine
3 — meeting a 6-ton T. rex? You don't have to
worry. T. rex died millions of years ago.

1. Writer starts with an interesting question.

2. Adjectives give a clear picture.

3. This is a strong ending.

4. Writer uses all the facts and adds own ideas.

Grammar Patrol

Grammar Patrol

adjective   An **adjective** describes a person, place, animal, or thing. An adjective can tell how something looks, sounds, tastes, feels, or smells.

- Some adjectives name **shapes.**

  I sit at a **round** desk.

- Some adjectives describe **size.** Words such as **big, small, long,** and **short** describe size.

  Mike ate a **big** piece of cake.

- Some adjectives name **colors.**

  I have a **red** coat.

- Some adjectives tell **how many.**

  The car has **four** doors.
  We invited **some** friends to the party.

- Some adjectives tell **what kind.**

  I heard a **loud** sound.
  The **funny** clown made faces.

- Add **–er** to an adjective to compare two persons, places, animals, or things.

  Mark is tall**er** than I am.   A rabbit is fast**er** than a turtle.

  Add **–est** to an adjective to compare three or more persons, places, animals, or things.

  Sarah is the tall**est** girl in the class.   Our school is the bigg**est** in town.

© Pearson Education

contraction A contraction is a short way to put two words together. A **verb** and the word **not** can be put together to make a contraction. An apostrophe (**'**) is used in place of the letter **o** in **not**.

are + not = aren't   has + not = hasn't
did + not = didn't   is + not = isn't
do + not = don't   was + not = wasn't
does + not = doesn't were + not = weren't

noun A **noun** names a person, a place, an animal, or a thing.

My **brother** sees a **zebra** at the **zoo**.
 (person) (animal) (place)

- Nouns can mean **more than one**. Many nouns add -**s** to mean **more than one**.

dinosaur + s = **dinosaurs**
crayon + s = **crayons**

- **nouns in sentences** A noun can be in more than one place in a sentence.

Bears live in **caves.**

© Pearson Education

- **proper nouns**   **Proper nouns** are special names for people, places, animals, and things. They begin with capital letters.

  Bill Fox plays on the baseball team.
  We went to **North Carolina.**

- A title can come before the name of a person. A title begins with a capital letter. Some titles end with a period (**.**).

  Our coach is **Mr. Wolf.**

- **Days of the week** begin with capital letters.

  Monday   Thursday   Sunday

- **Months of the year** begin with capital letters.

  March   June   November

- **Holidays** begin with capital letters.

  Thanksgiving   Memorial Day

pronoun   A **pronoun** is a word that takes the place of a noun or nouns. The words **I, he, she, it, we, you,** and **they** are pronouns. They are used in the naming part, or subject, of a sentence.

Miles and Sarah walked to school.

They walked to school.

Jake crosses the street.

He crosses the street.

© Pearson Education

- **Me, you, him, her, it, us,** and **them** are also pronouns. They are used in the action part, or predicate, of a sentence.

Laura draws **pictures**.   **She** draws **them**.

Dan meets **Dean** on the corner.   **He** meets **him** on the corner.

sentence   A sentence is a group of words that tells a complete idea. It begins with a capital letter.

My family went to a party.

- A sentence has a **naming part.** It names a person, place, animal, or thing. The naming part tells who or what the sentence is about.

Mary plants a flower.
The flower is yellow.

- A sentence has an **action part.** It tells what a person or thing does.

Jimmy **runs.**   He **races to the corner.**

- The **order** of the words in a sentence must make sense.

Beach is at the Peg.   These words are not in the right order.

Peg is at the beach.   These words are in the right order.

© Pearson Education

- A **telling sentence** tells something. It is a statement. A telling sentence begins with a capital letter. It usually ends with a **period (.)**.

  David plays the drums**.**

- A **question** is an asking sentence. It begins with a capital letter. It ends with a **question mark (?)**.

  Is that your bike**?**

- A **command** is a sentence that gives an order. It begins with a capital letter. It ends with a period **(.)**.

  Put the bowl on the table**.**

- An **exclamation** is a sentence that shows strong feeling. It begins with a **capital letter.** It ends with an **exclamation mark (!)**.

  What a great song that is**!**

- The meaning of a sentence changes if the word order changes.

  The **bag** is in the **box**.
  The **box** is in the **bag**.
  Is the **box** in the **bag**?

© Pearson Education

verb   A word that tells what someone or something does is a **verb.**

The girl **runs**.   The boy **skips.**

- A verb can tell what one person, animal, or thing does. Add **–s** to show what is being done now.

   Neil **reads** a book.   Yasmin **plays** the flute.

- Do not add **–s** to a verb that tells what two or more people, animals, or things do now.

   Tim and Tom **clean** their room.

- Verbs can tell what happened in the past. Some verbs that tell about the past end with **–ed.**

   Yesterday we **baked** cookies.

   (The verb **baked** tells about the past. It ends with **–ed.**)

- The verbs **am, is,** and **are** tell about now. Use **am** or **is** to tell about one. Use **are** to tell about more than one.

   I **am** a nurse.   Jose **is** a nurse.   Jo and Dan
   are nurses.

   The verbs **was** and **were** tell about the past. Use **was** to tell about one. Use **were** to tell about more than one.

   I **was** thirsty.   He **was** thirsty.   We **were** thirsty.

© Pearson Education

Capital Letters

sentence A sentence begins with a capital letter.

The cat is small.

names for people, places, and pets The names of people, places, and pets begin with capital letters.

Mary **S**mith and her dog **R**ex live in **B**oston.

titles for people Titles for people begin with capital letters. Most titles end with a period.

Ms. Chen talked to **Dr.** Jones and **Mr.** Smith.

days of the week The names of the days of the week begin with capital letters.

Our play is on **F**riday.

months and holidays The names of months and holidays begin with capital letters.

I know that **N**ew **Y**ear's **D**ay is in **J**anuary.

© Pearson Education

Punctuation

period   Use a period (**.**) at the end of a telling sentence.

Sue rides her bike**.**

- Use a period at the end of a command.

Go to sleep**.**

- Most titles for people end with a period.

Ms**.** Chen talked to Dr**.** Jones and Mr**.** Smith.

question mark   Use a question mark (**?**) at the end of an asking sentence, or question.

Where is your dog**?**

exclamation mark   Use an exclamation mark (**!**) at the end of an exclamation.

What a day we had**!**

© Pearson Education

apostrophe   Use an apostrophe (**'**) to take the place of the letter **o** in **not** in a contraction. A contraction is a short way to put two words together. A **verb** and the word **not** can be put together to make a contraction.

are + not = aren't   has + not = hasn't

© Pearson Education

Frequently Misspelled Words

For many writers, some words are difficult to spell. You can use this list to check your spelling.

A

a lot
about
again
all
always
and
another
are
as
away

B

baseball
be
beautiful
because
before
birthday
brother
but
by

C

came
caught
Christmas

come
could

D

didn't
different
do
does
don't
down

E

eat
end
every
everybody

F

family
favorite
find
first
for
found
friend
from

G

get
girl
give
go
going
good

H

Halloween
has
have
heard
her
here
him
his
home
house
how

I

I
into
is
it's

K

knew
know

L

like
little
live
look
love

M

make
many
more
my

N

new
nice
night
not
now

© Pearson Education

Frequently Misspelled Words

O

of
on
once
one
or
other
our
out
outside
over

P

part
party
people
play
presents
pretty
put

R

really

S

said
saw
scared
school
see
so
some
sometimes
special
started
swimming

T

thank
that
that's
the
their
them
then
there
there's
these

they
they're
thought
through
to
too
took
tried
two

U

under
upon
use

V

very

W

want
was
watch
we
went

were
what
when
where
who
whole
will
with
would

Y

you
your

© Pearson Education

D' Nealian™ Alphabet

a b c d e f g h i

j k l m n o p q r s t

u v w x y z

A B C D E F G

H I J K L M N O

P Q R S T U V

W X Y Z . , ' ?

1 2 3 4 5 6

7 8 9 10

© Pearson Education

Manuscript Alphabet

a b c d e f g

h i j k l m n

o p q r s t u

v w x y z

A B C D E F G

H I J K L M N

O P Q R S T U

V W X Y Z , ' . ?

1 2 3 4 5 6

7 8 9 10

© Pearson Education

Index

© Pearson Education

© Pearson Education

© Pearson Education

© Pearson Education

© Pearson Education

© Pearson Education

prompts, 26, 31, 36, 41, 55, 61, 67, 73, 79, 85, 91, 97, 103, 109, 115, 121, 127, 133, 139, 145, 151, 157, 163, 169, 175, 181, 187, 193, 199, 205, 211, 217, 223, 229, 232, 234, 236, 238, 240

put ideas in order, 6–7, 114

rhyme, 144

rules, 22–25

sentences, 18–21, 228

show, don't tell, 150

strong adjectives, 162

strong verbs, 126

supporting details, 216

tell what happens, 66

time-order words, 108

types of
descriptive, 31–35

expository, 41–45

narrative, 26–30

persuasive, 36–40

use commands in writing, 198

use exclamations in writing, 204

use nouns to describe, 90

use proper nouns in writing, 96

voice, 10–13, 54

word choice, 16–19, 192

words that tell how you feel, 78

write with nouns, 102

Writing for tests, 230–241

Writing models. *See* Writing.

© Pearson Education